CORPORATE DIRECTOR'S GUIDEBOOK

SIXTH EDITION

CORPORATE LAWS COMMITTEE

AMERICAN BAR ASSOCIATION
Business Law Section

Cover design by ABA Publishing.

Page Composition by Quadrum Solutions.

Printed in the United States of America.

18 17   8

Library of Congress Cataloging-in-Publication Data

Sale, Hillary A., 1961-, and Holly J. Gregory, editors
Corporate director's guidebook, 6th ed. / prepared by the Corporate Laws Committee of the Business Law Section of the American Bar Association
        p. cm.
    Rev. ed. of: Corporate director's guidebook / Committee on Corporate Laws. 5th ed. 2007.
    ISBN 978-1-61632-874-0 (alk. paper)
    1. Directors of corporations—Legal status, laws, etc.—United States. 2. Corporation law—United States. I. American Bar Association. Committee on Corporate Laws. II. Corporate director's guidebook. III. Title.
    KF1423.C67 2011
    346.73'066—dc22

                        2011010464

Contents

Foreword

This is the Sixth Edition of the Corporate Director's *Guidebook*. Since its initial publication in 1978, directors, business executives, advisors, students of corporate governance and others have all come to rely on the advice and commentary in the *Guidebook*. Indeed, the *Guidebook* is the most frequently cited handbook in its field.

The primary purpose of the *Guidebook* is to provide concise guidance to corporate directors in meeting their responsibilities. The *Guidebook* focuses on the role of the individual director, in the context of providing advice about the duties and operation of the board and its key committees (audit, nominating and governance, and compensation). Although many director decisions and tasks occur against a legal backdrop, we emphasize the law only in limited instances and otherwise attempt to avoid legalisms.

The Fifth Edition of the *Guidebook*, published in 2007, assumed that certain legal reforms like the Sarbanes-Oxley Act were a baseline for director action and focused on company performance under the spotlight of investor interests. This Sixth Edition is being published in the wake of the 2007–2010 financial crisis and the resulting legislation, the Dodd-Frank Wall Street Reform and Consumer Protection Act (Dodd-Frank Act). As a result, this edition emphasizes themes arising out of the crisis and important to all directors, particularly those in public companies.

The Sixth Edition explores the role of directors in overseeing both strategy and risk. Strategy and risk are interrelated, and directors cannot understand and guide strategy without also focusing on risk. Corporations must manage risks appropriately. Although not engaged in day-to-day risk management, directors are charged with its oversight.

Today, director decisions are subject to a much more significant level of public and shareholder scrutiny than ever before. To help directors engage in effective oversight and decision-making processes in the current environment, the Sixth Edition emphasizes the following:

- Risk management and its role in company strategy and operations;
- Executive compensation decision-making by compensation committees, with a focus on the links between compensation, performance and risk;
- Chief Executive Officer (CEO) succession planning and its relationship to strategy and risk oversight;
- Enhanced shareholder activism and power, including the pressure for proxy access in director elections; and
- New federal statutory and regulatory requirements that set forth legal baselines for boards and public companies.

The Sixth Edition also adds an appendix of corporate governance websites and blogs, as well as listings for associations, institutional investors and other resources.

The *Guidebook* provides important information for directors of public companies, but it is also relevant to directors of all companies in understanding their duties and obligations. In short, it provides a concise guide to boardroom best practices for all directors. The Corporate Laws Committee hopes directors and their advisors will benefit from this Sixth Edition of the *Guidebook*.

Respectfully submitted,

A. Gilchrist Sparks, III
Chair
Corporate Laws Committee

Corporate Laws Committee

The Corporate Laws Committee of the American Bar Association's Section of Business Law is composed of active or former practicing lawyers, law professors, regulators, and judges with corporate law expertise from throughout the United States and Canada. In addition to the *Corporate Director's Guidebook* and other scholarly writings, the Committee is responsible for the development of the *Model Business Corporation Act*.

The *Model Act*, first issued in 1950, has been adopted substantially in its entirety by more than 30 states in the United States and in important respects by many other states. The *Model Act* has played an important role in the development of corporate law in the United States and elsewhere.

The Committee serves as the permanent editorial board for the *Model Act*, reviewing, revising, and updating its provisions on a continuing basis. Moreover, the Committee publishes the *Model Business Corporation Act Annotated*, a comprehensive compilation of the *Model Act* and cases and authorities relevant to its provisions.

The roster of active Committee participants during the publication of the *Guidebook's* Sixth Edition (including appointed members, consultants, and liaisons from other ABA committees) is listed below.

James H. Cheek, III
Nashville, TN

William H. Clark, Jr.
Philadelphia, PA

Richard E. Climan
East Palo Alto, CA

John P. Coffey
Bronxville, NY

Professor James D. Cox
Durham, NC

Professor Michael P. Dooley
Charlottesville, VA

Karl J. Ege
Seattle, WA

Professor Lisa M. Fairfax
Washington, DC

Margaret M. Foran
Newark, NJ

Diane Holt Frankle
East Palo Alto, CA

Mark J. Gentile
Wilmington, DE

Allen Cunningham Goolsby
Richmond, VA

Holly J. Gregory
New York, NY

Carol Hansell
Toronto, Ontario

Whitney Holmes
Denver, CO

Mary Ann Jorgenson
Cleveland, OH

Eliot L. Kaplan
Phoenix, AZ

Stanley Keller
Boston, MA

Thomas J. Kim
Washington, DC

David B.H. Martin
Washington, DC

Michael R. McAlevey
Fairfield, CT

David C. McBride
Wilmington, DE

Thomas R. McNeill
Atlanta, GA

James P. Melican
Naples, FL

James C. Morphy
New York, NY

Patrick Pohlen
Menlo Park, CA

Steven A. Rosenblum
New York, NY

Kim K.W. Rucker
New York, NY

Professor Hillary A. Sale
St. Louis, MO

Larry P. Scriggins
Baltimore, MD

Marshall L. Small
San Francisco, CA

Laurie Smiley
Kirkland, WA

A. Gilchrist Sparks, III
Wilmington, DE

The Honorable
Leo E. Strine, Jr.

Wilmington, DE

Tina S. Van Dam
Midland, MI

The Honorable
E. Norman Veasey
Wilmington, DE

Robert M. Walmsley, Jr
New Orleans, LA

Herbert S. Wander
Chicago, IL

James B. Zimpritch
Portland, ME

Overview

This edition of the *Guidebook*, like its predecessors, explores the relationship of the board of directors to the CEO and other senior management officers as well as to shareholders. Directors are elected by the shareholders and have a duty to advance the interests of the corporation to the exclusion of their own interests. Shareholders do not have the right to manage the corporation. Instead, the board of directors oversees the business and affairs of the corporation and delegates to the officers the day-to-day operation of the enterprise. This book focuses on the balance in the allocation of rights and duties, emphasizing the ways in which directors of public corporations devote their time and experience to the strategy and oversight of the company's business.

The book is geared to the individual directors of public companies, or those with public shareholders and a trading market for their shares. The *Guidebook* is, however, relevant to all corporate directors. It provides an overview or guide to the role of the board, the functions and responsibilities of the board, and the board's structure, including committees and operations. The goal is to help directors be effective in fulfilling their duties to the corporation and in the boardroom.

Directors make many decisions on a regular basis. In doing so, they must apply their business judgment based on reasonably available material information and act in what they reasonably believe to be the best interests of the corporation. In some cases, a board may even make a decision, in good faith, knowing that a substantial percentage of shareholders might disagree with that decision.

In today's world, most directors are "independent directors." The key challenge for directors is to oversee the corporation's activities and strategy by utilizing effective oversight processes and making informed decisions, without becoming day-to-day managers. In doing so, directors must be cognizant of their obligation to act free of conflicts and in what they perceive to be the best interests of all shareholders. This *Guidebook* helps directors meet that responsibility by explaining how they can exercise their oversight and decision-making responsibilities and by identifying the boardroom practices and procedures that support and promote effective director involvement.

> *The key challenge for directors is to oversee the corporation's activities and strategy by utilizing effective oversight processes and making informed decisions, without becoming day-to-day managers. This* Guidebook *helps directors meet that responsibility by explaining how they can exercise their oversight and decision-making responsibilities and by identifying the boardroom practices and procedures that support and promote effective director involvement.*

Importantly, directors exercise their decision-making powers only by acting collectively, either as a board or as a board committee. Judgment, however, is exercised individually, and informed judgment requires individual preparation and participation, as well as group deliberation. Effective board oversight results from both group deliberation and from the recognition by an individual that a particular matter warrants further inquiry or action.

Corporations are creatures of the state in which they are incorporated. For corporate directors and the corporation itself, that means that the statutes and state court decisions of the state of incorporation will govern many corporate decisions and processes. The same is true of judicial decisions. Public corporations, however, are also subject to federal securities laws and regulations and the listing standards of the major securities markets. The *Guidebook* addresses the federal securities law regime and the listing standards that mandate specific governance processes. The *Guidebook* does not, however, address industry-specific federal or state regimes, such as, for example, regulations applicable to financial institutions or utilities.

Importantly, most directors are not lawyers, and, as a result, where appropriate, they should seek legal advice to ensure they satisfy legal requirements and properly support the board's deliberative decision-making processes. Although not all corporations have an internal general counsel, for convenience, the *Guidebook* uses the term "general counsel" to refer to both internal and external lawyers who fulfill that role.

Importantly, most directors are not lawyers, and, as a result, where appropriate, they should seek legal advice to ensure they satisfy legal requirements and properly support the board's deliberative decision-making processes.

Joining a Board of Directors

Joining a board and serving as a director can and should be a challenging, exciting, and rewarding experience. Board service entails significant responsibilities and requires a significant personal investment of time and attention. Directors must fulfill fiduciary duties of care and loyalty. Because directors put their reputations at stake, the decision whether to join a board should not be made casually.

An individual considering an invitation to join a board should carefully study the corporation, its business, its history, its board, and its senior management. The candidate should understand the reasons for the invitation and the board's expectations. For example, would the candidate be expected to serve in a particular role on the board or any of its committees—perhaps as a member of the nominating and governance committee or as a designated "financial expert" on the audit committee?

An individual considering an invitation to join a board should carefully study the corporation, its business, its history, its board, and its senior management. The candidate should understand the reasons for the invitation and the board's expectations.

The discussion in this *Guidebook* focuses on public company directors. Most directors of private corporations will likely have some ownership interest in or connection to the corporation, its founder or its owners. If asked to join the board of a private company or a closely controlled company, an individual should explore the expected role of an outsider on the board and

understand the corporation's shareholder base (including any fac-
tions among the shareholders), its business, its reputation and its
legal profile. In addition, the candidate should understand the
directors' relationships with the shareholders; determine whether independent legal judgment is really desired and whether
advice will be available if requested (and, if so, from whom);
inquire whether an initial public offering of the corporation is
contemplated; and consider taking some of the steps described
in the following list, such as reviewing the corporation's
financial information and becoming familiar with its director and
officer insurance coverage.

When asked to join the board of a public company, an individual should first assess the following:

- whether the opportunity to serve on the board is sufficiently compelling to engage the individual's serious interest
and attention in light of competing commitments;
- whether the individual has (i) sufficient time and flexibility
to perform diligently the required duties for a director of
that company, including if a corporate crisis or major transaction should arise; (ii) scheduling conflicts that would
unduly interfere with the board's normal meeting schedule; (iii) requisite skills and experience to participate
meaningfully as a director of that company; and (iv) any
present, foreseeable, or perceived conflicts of interest with
the corporation, its business or its senior management (*e.g.*,
material relationships with competitors, potential acquisition targets, potential acquirers, or close personal or
business ties to the CEO, other directors, or other senior
members of the management team);
- whether the individual has or can develop a sufficient
depth of understanding of the corporation's business,
business model, and competitive environment to be an
effective director; and
- whether the individual believes that senior management
and the board have integrity and conduct themselves in an
honest and ethical manner.

A candidate still interested in the opportunity and
who believes that she or he has the ability to be an effective

director and add value to the corporation, should take the following steps:

- meet with the nominating/corporate governance committee chair, board chair, lead director and/or other board representatives who extended the invitation, and with the CEO and other senior members of management, to discuss the corporation's strategy, principal issues, board organization and procedures and committee memberships contemplated for the individual;
- assess the attitude of the CEO and senior management toward shareholder accountability and board activity to determine whether a proactive board and independent director judgment are truly desired;
- review the corporation's recent public disclosure documents, such as press releases, investor presentations, and SEC filings to learn about the corporation, including the nature of its business, its financial condition, risk factors, and stability of its current business activities and future prospects;
- determine whether there are company- or industry-specific factors requiring special understanding or attention— for example, a financially challenged or distressed corporation may require specialized experience or an unusual time commitment, or a company facing serious competition or cyclic challenges may benefit from particular expertise; and
- gather information about the corporation's reputation in the investment community and in the business world generally, by reviewing press and analyst reports and conducting Internet and other searches.

If, following preliminary diligence, the individual understands the corporation's strategy, business activities, risks, culture and prospects, and has a continuing and serious interest in the directorship opportunity, she or he should take these additional steps:

- learn the structure and processes the board uses to provide effective oversight, including (i) the corporation's corporate governance principles or guidelines and committee charters; (ii) the routine operation of the board and its committees, including its access to and interface with the CEO, CFO, and other senior management officers; (iii) the methods employed for monitoring and evaluating board and committee performance; (iv) the tone and culture of executive sessions of independent directors; (v) the "tone at the top" for integrity and diligence; and (vi) the procedures for appointments, evaluation, and succession planning related to senior executive officers, including the CEO;

- review the audit committee's membership and procedures and meet with the audit committee chair to discuss any recent or current critical financial or accounting issues (including rating agency concerns, if any), the clarity and transparency of public disclosures respecting the corporation's financial affairs, and the effectiveness of the corporation's programs to address risk management and legal compliance issues;
- review recent examples of the "meeting book" provided to directors in advance of meetings and other information regularly provided to the directors;
- identify the corporation's regular internal and external legal and financial advisors and learn their role and participation in and availability to the corporation's and the board's activities;
- understand, based on appropriate professional advice, the corporation's director exculpation, indemnification, and litigation expense advancement provisions (in organizational documents and contracts) and the amount and scope of coverage provided by the corporation's directors' and officers' liability insurance, the quality of the corporation's insurance carrier(s), and whether the corporation has provided the outside directors with separate insurance;
- request a briefing on significant claims or litigation against the corporation, especially any that involve the activities of the board of directors or involve any entity with which the prospective director is already affiliated; and
- understand director compensation arrangements and determine whether they are commensurate with the effort required and the risk undertaken.

The corporation may require a confidentiality commitment from the candidate covering the disclosure of any non-public information regarding the corporation's business and affairs. The corporation typically reimburses reasonable out-of-pocket expenses, such as travel expenses, incurred in the due diligence process.

When serving on a board, directors often value most the opportunity to collaborate on tough issues with other experienced business people who bring a wide variety of approaches, styles, and experience to boardroom deliberations. Directors must be able to work toward building consensus on issues. To facilitate this collaboration and decision-making process, directors must be able to formulate and articulate their views and engage in constructive dialogue in an atmosphere of candor, mutual respect, and confidentiality. Accordingly, in addition to the diligence steps outlined above, a candidate should attempt to assess the board's collegiality and culture of constructive skepticism, to the extent feasible from an outsider's perspective.

> *When serving on a board, directors often value most the opportunity to collaborate on tough issues with other experienced business people who bring a wide variety of approaches, styles, and experience to boardroom deliberations. Directors must be able to work toward building consensus on issues. To facilitate this collaboration and decision-making process, directors must be able to formulate and articulate their views and engage in constructive dialogue in an atmosphere of candor, mutual respect, and confidentiality.*

Responsibilities, Rights, and Duties of a Corporate Director

Directors have a responsibility to act in the best interests of the corporation and its shareholders. To do so, they must focus on maximizing the value of the corporation for the benefit of its shareholders. Directors fulfill this responsibility through two primary board functions: decision-making and oversight. The board's decision-making function generally involves considering and, if warranted, approving corporate policy and strategic goals and taking specific actions such as evaluating and selecting top management, approving major expenditures and transactions and acquiring and disposing of material assets. The board's oversight function involves monitoring the corporation's business and affairs including, for example, financial performance, management performance, compliance with legal obligations and corporate policies, and evaluating appropriate risk management structures. Both functions require that directors develop an understanding of the corporation's business and the environment in which it operates, including the risks and opportunities it faces, and management's capacity to run the business while managing risks. In addition, directors need to ensure that they have sufficient information to engage in informed decision-making and oversight.

Although the board is responsible for managing and overseeing corporate affairs, it typically delegates responsibility for day-to-day operations to a team of professional managers. Management has responsibility for such tasks. Directors must oversee the corporation's activities effectively and make informed decisions without usurping the role of management.

Directors have, individually and collectively, various responsibilities and rights, described more fully in the next section. Directors should keep in mind that, aside from specific tasks that the board delegates to board committees, the board acts as a collective body. Further, even for delegated tasks, the board must continue to provide oversight. Directors must, however, exercise judgment on an individual basis, and informed judgment depends upon each director's individual evaluation, preparation, and participation, as well as on group deliberation and interaction.

Federal laws and regulations, the listing standards of national securities markets, as well as judicial interpretations of state laws, have all increased the compliance and disclosure obligations for the board and management of public companies. These obligations do not, however, change the fundamental principles governing director action.

> *Federal laws and regulations, the listing standards of national securities markets, as well as judicial interpretations of state laws, have all increased the compliance and disclosure obligations for the board and management of public companies.*

A. Board Responsibilities

State corporate statutes define the relationship between the board and management of the corporation. In general, state laws provide that all corporate powers shall be exercised by or under the authority of the corporation's board of directors, and its business and affairs shall be managed by or under the direction of, and subject to the oversight of, the board. Thus, typically, the board delegates management to officers and is then responsible for overseeing the corporation while management conducts the corporation's daily affairs.

State corporate statutes emphasize the board's responsibility to make major decisions on behalf of the corporation and to oversee the management of the corporation. Although these statutes do not specifically define board responsibilities, the following tasks are generally undertaken by the board and its committees:

- monitoring the corporation's performance in light of its operating, financial, and other significant corporate plans, strategies, and objectives, and approving major changes in plans and strategies;
- selecting the CEO, setting goals for the CEO and other senior executives, reviewing their performance, evaluating and establishing their compensation, and making changes when appropriate;
- developing, approving, and implementing succession plans for the CEO and top senior executives;
- understanding the corporation's risk profile and reviewing and overseeing the corporation's management of risks;
- understanding the corporation's financial statements and other financial disclosures and monitoring the adequacy of its financial and other internal controls, as well as its disclosure controls and procedures;
- evaluating and approving major transactions such as mergers, acquisitions, significant expenditures, and the disposition of major assets; and
- establishing and monitoring effective systems for receiving and reporting information about the corporation's compliance with its legal and ethical obligations.

As the foregoing reveals, the board's principal responsibilities are to select the top management for the corporation, plan for succession, and provide general direction and guidance with respect to the corporation's strategy and management's conduct of the business. In so doing, the board should give significant consideration to the corporation's financial and business objectives, as well as its risk profile.

In recent years, the average tenure of a CEO has fallen, making succession planning important, both for unexpected emergencies and with the long term in mind. Boards must develop, approve, and implement succession plans for the CEO and top senior executives. Some corporations establish separate succession planning committees, and in others, succession planning is a matter for the compensation or nominating committee or the full board. There is no "one size fits all" model for succession planning, but the board should take an active role in assessing on an ongoing basis whether the current senior management team is appropriate for the needs of the organization, as well as in implementing and periodically reviewing management development and succession plans. Through this process, boards gain the knowledge required to develop judgment about the corporation's potential future leaders.

The board safeguards the corporation's integrity and reputation. The CEO and senior management must take the leadership role to promote integrity, honesty, and ethical conduct throughout the organization. The board's role is to assess the CEO's commitment and efforts in this area, support and encourage appropriate values (including through policies and incentives), and provide oversight of the programs and procedures that management implements to support behaviors and identify issues that may arise (including reporting mechanisms). This board role includes directing the CEO and other members of the senior management team to establish the proper "tone at the top" by setting clear expectations for the corporation's ethical behavior and conduct of its business in compliance with law.

A number of state corporation statutes expressly allow the board to consider the interests of employees, suppliers, and customers, as well as the communities in which the corporation operates and the environment. Of course, the board remains accountable primarily to shareholders for the performance of the corporation. Thus, non-shareholder constituency considerations are best understood not as independent corporate objectives but as factors to be considered in pursuing the best interests of the corporation. Indeed, being responsive to stakeholder interests and concerns can contribute

Being responsive to stakeholder interests and concerns can contribute positively to corporate valuation, workplace culture and reputation for integrity and ethical behavior.

positively to corporate valuation, workplace culture and reputation for integrity and ethical behavior.

Increasingly, boards—and, as directed, board committees—engage in periodic communications with shareholders. Board efforts to enhance shareholder communication and dialogue require sensitivity to director confidentiality requirements, as well as federal regulations on "selective" disclosure. In light of such obligations, individual directors should understand and abide by the board's policies on confidentiality and selective disclosure and avoid responding to shareholder inquiries or communicating with any shareholders. Instead, shareholder communication and engagement should be undertaken on a coordinated and not an *ad hoc* basis.

B. Individual Responsibilities

To be effective, a director must understand the corporation's business, operations, and competitive environment. This knowledge is fundamental to the director's ability to form an objective judgment about corporate and senior management performance and strategic direction, and to challenge, support, and reward management as warranted. Accordingly, a director's understanding of the corporation and its industry should include:

- the corporation's business plan;
- the key drivers underlying the corporation's profitability and cash flow—how the corporation makes money both as a whole and also in its significant business segments;
- the corporation's operational and financial plans, strategies, and objectives and how they further the goal of enhancing shareholder value;
- the corporation's economic, financial, regulatory, and competitive risks, as well as risks to the corporation's physical assets, intellectual property, personnel, and reputation;
- the corporation's financial condition and the results of its operations and those of its significant business segments for recent periods; and
- the corporation's performance compared with that of its competitors.

In addition, a director should be satisfied that effective systems exist for timely reporting to, and consideration by, the board or relevant board committees of the following:

- corporate objectives and strategic plans;
- current business and financial performance of the corporation and its significant business segments, as compared to board-approved objectives and plans;
- material risk and liability contingencies, including industry risk, current and threatened litigation, and regulatory matters; and
- systems of company controls designed to manage risk and to provide reasonable assurance of compliance with law and corporate policies.

Directors should do their homework so that they are prepared to participate actively. In addition to attending board and committee meetings, they should review board and committee agendas and related materials sufficiently in advance of meetings to enable them to participate actively in the deliberative process. Directors should expect to receive drafts of minutes of board and committee meetings in a reasonably prompt time frame, so that they can assure that minutes accurately reflect their recollections of what occurred at meetings and that identified active items are being pursued. Directors should also keep informed about the activities of board committees on which they do not serve.

Directors should have an attitude of constructive skepticism. Directors should not be reticent or passive. To be a director means to direct — to participate on an informed basis, ask questions, challenge management as appropriate, apply considered business judgment to matters brought before the board, and when necessary, bring other matters to the full board's attention.

More generally, directors should have an attitude of constructive skepticism. Directors should not be reticent or passive. To be a director means to direct—to participate on an informed basis, ask questions, challenge management as appropriate, apply considered business judgment to matters brought before the board, and when necessary, bring other matters to the full board's attention.

Each director works for the benefit of the corporation—even if nominated or designated by a subset of the shareholder body (*e.g.*, holders of preferred stock who may have special rights to elect a director), elected in a proxy contest, or appointed by the board to fill a vacancy. Directors may consider the interests of particular shareholders when performing their decision-making and oversight duties, but all directors must act in the best interests of the corporation and all of its shareholders.

C. Rights

Because of important business decision and oversight responsibilities, all directors have both legal and customary rights of access to the information and resources needed to do the job. Among the most important are the rights:

- to inspect books and records;
- to request additional information reasonably necessary to exercise informed oversight and make careful decisions;
- to inspect facilities as reasonably appropriate to gain an understanding of corporate operations;
- to receive timely notice of all meetings in which a director is entitled to participate;
- to receive copies of key documents and of all board and committee meeting minutes; and
- to receive regular oral or written reports of the activities of all board committees.

In addition, within reasonable time and manner constraints, directors generally have the right of access to key executives and other employees of the corporation and to the corporation's legal counsel and other advisors to obtain information relevant to the performance of their duties. Directors may (and should) request that any issue of concern be put on the board (or appropriate committee) agenda.

The right to information is accompanied by the duty to keep corporate information confidential and not to misuse information for personal benefit or for the benefit of others. For example, individual directors do not have the right to share confidential information with shareholders who nominate or elect them—unless they have express authority from the board (and subject to selective disclosure and insider trading prohibitions).

The board and its committees should expect the general counsel, if there is one, to be available as a resource to advise them. Correspondingly, the general counsel must recognize that the client is the corporation, as represented by the board of directors, and not the CEO or any other officer or group of managers. The board and board committees should have access to the corporation's regular outside counsel, if one exists, and the authority to retain their own legal counsel and professional advisors, independent of those who usually advise the corporation. Indeed, the Sarbanes-Oxley Act and the Dodd-Frank Act both grant specific committees the right to engage counsel and advisors. The chapters on individual committees address these issues.

D. Legal Obligations

The baseline legal standard for director conduct is that each director must discharge director duties in good faith and in a manner that the director reasonably believes to be in the best interests of the corporation. This standard encompasses a "duty of care" and a "duty of loyalty." To satisfy the duty of care, a director must act with the care that a person in a like position would reasonably believe appropriate under similar circumstances. The duty of loyalty focuses on avoidance (or appropriate handling) of conflicts of interests, and requires fair dealing by directors involved in transactions that result or could result in personal or financial conflicts with the corporation. The duty of loyalty also requires directors to act in good faith. A lack of good faith would include (i) acting intentionally with a purpose other than that of advancing the best interests of the corporation, (ii) acting with the intent to violate applicable law, or (iii) failing to act in the face of a known duty to act in a manner that demonstrates conscious disregard of, or extreme inattention to, the director's duties.

1. Duty of Care

A director's duty of care primarily relates to the responsibility to become and remain reasonably informed in making decisions and overseeing the corporation's business. As noted above, directors satisfy their duty of care when they act with the care that a person in a like position would reasonably believe appropriate under similar circumstances. This "reasonable belief" incorporates a director's personal belief, but it also must be based upon a rational analysis of the situation as understandable to others. The phrase "like position" means that a director's actions must incorporate the basic attributes of common sense, practical wisdom, and informed judgment generally associated with the position of corporate director. The phrase "under similar circumstances" recognizes that the nature and extent of the preparation for and deliberations leading up to decision-making, and the level of oversight, vary depending on the corporation's circumstances and the nature of the decision to be made.

In particular, satisfying the duty of care requires that directors have all material information reasonably available. Directors generally meet this standard by attending meetings, reading materials and otherwise preparing in advance of meetings, asking questions of management or advisors, requesting legal or other expert advice when desirable for a board decision, and bringing the director's own knowledge and experience to bear. To meet the duty of care, directors should consider the following:

a. Time commitment and regular attendance

Directors should commit the required time to prepare for, attend regularly, and participate in board and committee meetings. By state law, directors may not participate or vote by proxy; personal participation is required. Directors who are physically present at a meeting have the opportunity to engage in spontaneous interactions that occur before, during, and after the meeting, and are more aware of the group's dynamics. Personal participation may also take place by telephone or other means of communication by which all directors can hear each other.

b. Need to be informed and prepared

Directors must take appropriate steps to be informed. Without sufficient information, directors cannot participate meaningfully or fulfill their duties effectively. In most cases, the best source of information about the corporation is management. Directors can ask management to be present at board or committee meetings. To be informed and prepared directors should:

- ensure that management provides directors with sufficient information about the corporation's business and affairs;
- request additional information when appropriate; and
- ask questions to ensure that they understand the information provided.

Directors should establish expectations with respect to management provision of sufficient information in a timely manner. If management is unresponsive or otherwise fails to satisfy such expectations, the board should consider taking action including, in appropriate circumstances, replacing management. When contemplating specific actions, directors should receive the relevant information far enough in advance of the board or committee meeting to be able to study and reflect on the issues. Important, time-sensitive materials that become available between meetings should be promptly distributed to directors. Directors should review carefully the materials supplied. If a director believes that information is insufficient or inaccurate, or is not made available in a timely manner, the director should request that action be delayed until appropriate information is available and can be studied. If expert advice would be needed for a decision, the director should request that the board seek such advice.

c. Right to rely on others

In discharging board or committee duties, directors may rely in good faith on reports, opinions, information, and statements (including financial statements and other financial data) from:

- corporate officers or employees whom the director reasonably believes to be reliable and competent in the matters presented;
- legal counsel, public accountants, or other persons as to matters that the director reasonably believes to be within their professional or expert competence or as to which the person otherwise merits confidence; and
- committees of the board on which the director does not serve.

Such reliance is permissible unless the director has knowledge that would make the reliance unwarranted. Delegation to a committee does not relieve a director of oversight responsibility. Instead, a director should keep informed about committee and board activities.

Directors also implicitly rely on each other's statements, good faith, and judgment in making decisions for the corporation's benefit. Reliance is particularly likely when some directors have substantial experience or expertise in an area germane to the corporation's business—for example, by having specialized knowledge about a particular industry. Directors are expected to use their knowledge, experience, and special expertise for the benefit of all directors and the corporation generally.

> *Directors are expected to use their knowledge, experience, and special expertise for the benefit of all directors and the corporation generally.*

Obtaining input from competent advisors is a hallmark of a careful decision-making process. For this reason, directors who rely in good faith on advisors, professionals, and other persons with particular expertise or competence generally enjoy broad protections from liability. Nevertheless, reliance is appropriate only if directors reasonably believe that the advice is within the person's area of competence and if they selected that person with reasonable care. Directors have the final responsibility for their actions.

d. Inquiry

Directors should inquire into potential problems or issues when alerted by circumstances or events suggesting that board attention is appropriate. For example, inquiry is warranted when information appears materially inaccurate or inadequate, when there is reason to question the competence, loyalty or candor of management or of an advisor, or when common sense calls for it under the circumstances. When directors have information indicating that the corporation is or may be experiencing significant problems in a particular area of business or may be engaging in potentially unlawful or unethical conduct, they should promptly make further inquiry and follow up until they are reasonably satisfied that management is dealing with the situation appropriately. Even when there are no "red flags," directors should satisfy themselves periodically that the corporation maintains information systems and procedures that are appropriately designed to identify and manage compliance and business risks and are reasonably effective in maintaining compliance with laws and corporate policies and procedures.

> *When directors have information indicating that the corporation is or may be experiencing significant problems in a particular area of business or may be engaging in potentially unlawful or unethical conduct, they should promptly make further inquiry and follow up until they are reasonably satisfied that management is dealing with the situation appropriately.*

e. Candor among directors

Candid discussion among directors and between directors and management is critical to effective board decision-making. Generally, directors must inform other directors and management about information material to corporate decisions of which they are aware. Directors occasionally also have legal or other duties of confidentiality owed to another corporation or entity. In such a situation, a director should seek legal advice regarding the director's obligations, including reporting confidentiality obligations to the other directors and not participating in consideration of the matter.

2. Duty of Loyalty

The duty of loyalty requires directors to act in good faith and in the best interests of the corporation—and not in their own interests or in the interests of another person (*e.g.*, a family member or potential competitor) or organization with which they are associated. There are many situations in which loyalty to the corporation is an issue. These situations fall into two basic categories. The first involves situations where directors' personal or financial interests conflict with the corporation's, and the second involves disloyalty to the corporation for reasons other than personal or financial conflicts of interest.

a. Acting in good faith

The fundamental requirement of loyalty is that directors must act with the good faith belief that their actions are in the best interests of the corporation. Directors fail to act in good faith when they are disloyal either because their actions are motivated by bad faith or because they intentionally or knowingly disregarded their duties or responsibilities. Directors may fail to act in good faith in a variety of ways, including the following:

- intentionally acting with a purpose other than advancing the corporation's best interests;
- failing to act when there is a known duty to act;
- acting with the intent to violate, or with intentional disregard of, an applicable law;
- failing to cause the corporation to establish internal controls, risk management, or monitoring and compliance systems; or
- failing to respond to red flags.

b. Conflicts of interest

Directors should not use their position for personal profit or gain or for any other personal or non-corporate advantage. They should seek to avoid conflicts of interest and should take special care to disclose potential conflicts and handle appropriately any conflicts that may arise. Directors should be alert and sensitive to any interest they may have that might conflict with the best interests of the corporation, and they should disclose such interests to the designated board representative or committee and the general counsel.

> *Directors should not use their position for personal profit or gain or for any other personal or non-corporate advantage. They should seek to avoid conflicts of interest and should take special care to disclose potential conflicts and handle appropriately any conflicts that may arise.*

When directors have a direct or indirect financial or personal interest in a matter before the board for decision—including a contract or transaction to which the corporation is to be a party, or which involves the use of corporate assets, or which may involve competition with the corporation—they are considered "interested" in the matter. Interested directors should disclose the interest to the board members who are to act on the matter and disclose the relevant facts concerning it. Directors should refrain from engaging in any transaction with the corporation unless directors who do not share the conflict ("disinterested directors") or disinterested shareholders approve the transaction after full disclosure of the conflict or the underlying action is demonstrably fair (and can be proved so in court if challenged).

Sometimes a conflict arises from a corporation's plan to do business with an entity with which a director has a preexisting relationship. Upon learning of such a conflict, the director should fully disclose the relationship and other pertinent information. If the confidentiality obligations a director owes to a third party impair or proscribe full disclosure, a director may not be able to discharge the duties to the corporation and may need to recuse himself or herself from all participation concerning the matter, or even to resign.

In most situations, after disclosing the interest, describing the relevant facts, and responding to any questions, the interested director should leave the meeting while the disinterested directors complete their deliberations. This enables the disinterested directors to discuss the matter without being (or creating the appearance of being) influenced by the presence of the interested director. A director should generally abstain from voting on matters in which she or he has a conflict of interest. Disclosures of conflicts of interest and the results of the disinterested directors' consideration of the matter should be documented in minutes or reports. In some cases, a special committee of disinterested directors to review and pass on the transaction may be appropriate.

Conflicting interest transactions are sometimes unavoidable and are not inherently improper. Disinterested directors or shareholders, with full disclosure of material information about the transaction, may authorize these transactions. State corporation statutes usually provide specific procedures for authorizing or ratifying interested director transactions. Those procedures safeguard both the corporation and any interested director, and protect the enforceability of any action taken. Otherwise, if the transaction is challenged, the interested director must establish the entire fairness of the transaction to the corporation, judged according to circumstances at the time of the commitment.

A transaction between a director, or the director's immediate family, and the corporation is a "related person" transaction under the federal securities laws and may require disclosure in the corporation's annual report, proxy statement, or other public filings. Even if the transaction does not require public disclosure, the corporation may be required to disclose in general terms whether the board considered the transaction in determining whether the director is an "independent" director under market listing standards. In addition, corporations may have their own policies in these areas. Waiving such a policy for a director may trigger a disclosure obligation. Directors should be familiar with these disclosure requirements and related corporate policies. Disinterested directors should consider the ramifications of any disclosures when voting on a matter involving a director conflict.

c. Fairness to the corporation

Disinterested directors reviewing the fairness of a transaction involving conflict of interest or self-dealing elements should seek to determine (i) whether the terms of the proposed transaction are at least as favorable to the corporation and its shareholders as might be available from unrelated persons or entities; (ii) whether the proposed transaction is reasonably likely to further the corporation's business activities; and (iii) whether the process by which the decision is approved or ratified is fair. If the transaction could adversely affect shareholders, the directors should be especially concerned that those shareholders receive fair treatment. This concern increases when one or more directors or a dominant shareholder or shareholder group has a divergent or conflicting interest.

d. Independent advice

Independent advice regarding the merits of a conflict of interest or related person transaction is generally helpful. This advice may be contained (i) in oral or written fairness opinions, appraisals, or valuations by investment bankers or appraisers; (ii) in legal advice or opinions on various issues; or (iii) in analyses, reports or recommendations by other relevant experts.

e. Corporate opportunity

The duty of loyalty is also implicated when an opportunity related to the business of the corporation, including its subsidiaries and affiliates, becomes available to a director. Directors must typically make such opportunities available to the corporation before they may pursue them. Whether directors must first offer an opportunity to the corporation will depend on factors such as whether the opportunity is similar to the corporation's existing or contemplated business, the circumstances under which the director learned of the opportunity, and whether the corporation has an interest or expectancy in the opportunity.

If a director has reason to believe that a contemplated transaction might be a corporate opportunity, the director should bring it to the attention of the board and disclose the material information that the director knows about the opportunity. If the board, acting through its disinterested directors, disclaims interest in the opportunity on behalf of the corporation, then the director is free to pursue it.

3. Business Judgment Rule

Judicial review of challenged decisions will normally be governed by the "business judgment rule." The business judgment rule is not a description of a duty or a standard for determining whether a breach of duty has occurred. It is a standard of judicial review used to analyze director conduct to determine whether a board decision can be challenged or a director will be personally liable.

The business judgment rule is not a description of a duty or a standard for determining whether a breach of duty has occurred. It is a standard of judicial review used to analyze director conduct to determine whether a board decision can be challenged or a director will be personally liable.

The business judgment rule presumes that in making a business decision, independent and disinterested directors acted on an informed basis, in good faith, and in the honest belief that the action taken was in the best interests of the corporation. The rule applies to suits by shareholders acting for themselves or derivatively on behalf of the corporation. The court will determine only whether the directors making the decision were independent and disinterested in the matter, informed themselves before taking the action, and acted in the good faith belief that the decision was in the best interests of the corporation. If so, the court will not second-guess the decision and the directors will be protected from personal liability to the corporation and its shareholders—even if the board's decision turns out to be unwise or the results of the decision are unsuccessful. Importantly, the business judgment rule protects only decisions whether to take or not to take action. It does not, however, protect the failure to take action or conduct implicating breaches of the duty of loyalty.

4. Duty of Disclosure

Directors should never mislead or misinform shareholders. In addition, directors have an obligation to furnish shareholders with all relevant material information when presenting shareholders with a voting or investment decision. Directors also have a duty to inform fellow directors and management about information known to the director that is relevant to corporate decisions.

5. Confidentiality

A director must keep confidential all matters involving the corporation that have not been disclosed to the public. Directors must be aware of the corporation's confidentiality, insider trading, and disclosure policies and comply with them. Although a public company director may receive inquiries from major shareholders, media, analysts, or friends to comment on sensitive issues, individual directors should avoid responding to such inquiries, particularly when confidential or market-sensitive information is involved. Instead, they should refer requests for information to the CEO or other designated spokesperson.

> *A director must keep confidential all matters involving the corporation that have not been disclosed to the public. Directors must be aware of the corporation's confidentiality, insider trading, and disclosure policies and comply with them.*

A director who improperly discloses non-public information to persons outside the corporation can, for example, harm the corporation's competitive position or damage investor relations and, if the information is material, incur personal liability as a tipper of inside information or cause the corporation to violate federal securities laws. Equally important, unauthorized director disclosure of non-public information can damage the bond of trust between and among directors and management, discourage candid discussions, and jeopardize boardroom effectiveness and director collaboration.

E. Sale Transactions and Election Contests

The board of directors establishes a corporation's long-term business strategy and the time frame for achieving corporate goals. Directors may consider the relative merits of various alternatives for the corporation over the short, medium, or long term.

The sale of the corporation is one of the most important matters boards consider. An outright sale of the company for cash ends the shareholders' ownership of the business. A sale of the corporation for stock changes the form and substance of the shareholders' investment in the business. Directors should consider not only the potential value of the transaction to shareholders (compared with other alternatives reasonably available to the corporation over a reasonable time frame), but also the risks inherent in the transaction, including the risk that the transaction will not close. If the transaction is publicly announced but is delayed or not completed, the corporation risks losing valuable employees and disrupting relationships with key customers and suppliers. Although every sale transaction presents this risk, directors should consider the relative likelihood of events that might result in delay or failure to close, such as regulatory issues, as well as the possible mitigation of these risks.

> *Directors should consider not only the potential value of the transaction to shareholders (compared with other alternatives reasonably available to the corporation over a reasonable time frame), but also the risks inherent in the transaction, including the risk that the transaction will not close.*

Before deciding to sell the corporation, the directors must seek the best reasonably available price and terms and may need to put protective measures in place to help achieve their goals. There is no single blueprint a board should follow to obtain the best price and terms. In most cases, the board should engage experienced advisors familiar with customary terms, market conditions, and the legal and financial issues involved.

A potential sale of the corporation may present conflicts of interest for directors and officers who stand to benefit from change-of-control provisions or who have pre-existing relationships with one or more potential acquirers or will become part of the acquiring group. In this situation, the board can continue to act with the interested directors absenting themselves from the discussion. If an interested party is in a position to control the decision, a court may review the transaction to determine whether it is fair to the corporation and its disinterested shareholders. Where potential conflicts of interest are present, it is prudent to have independent and disinterested directors—who are empowered to engage independent, qualified advisors—handle negotiations with the interested party. The corporation will also have enhanced disclosure obligations under federal and state law in connection with a potential sale of the corporation, including any golden parachutes or compensation provisions with certain senior executive officers.

Similarly, as addressed in Section 10, directors generally have enhanced disclosure and legal obligations in connection with election contests. Because these situations have the potential to raise various strategic and financial issues, as well as complicated legal issues, directors should obtain advice from experienced counsel and qualified financial advisors.

F. Financial Distress Situations

The directors of a corporation facing potential default on obligations or bankruptcy must make decisions not encountered by the directors of financially healthy companies. Although directors' general responsibilities continue to apply, circumstances of severe financial distress can alter corporate goals and enhance creditors' rights vis-à-vis the corporation. If a corporation is in financial distress, the corporation should consider decisions regarding dividends and other distributions, recapitalizations, reorganizations, and other major corporate actions only with the benefit of legal advice from experienced counsel.

Insolvency is a legally significant status of financial distress. A corporation may be considered insolvent where the fair value of the corporation's liabilities exceeds the fair value of its assets. Insolvency also may exist if the corporation is not able to pay its debts as they fall due in the ordinary course of business. Directors should seek the advice of management if they are uncertain whether the corporation is solvent and, when appropriate, hire experienced counsel and other advisors to provide advice on the matter.

Insolvency generally gives rise to additional legal protections to creditors. The laws of most states and the U.S. Bankruptcy Code prohibit transactions that may prejudice creditors' ability to obtain payment from the corporation. A corporation may be liable under these laws if it is in financial distress and transfers assets of value without receiving reasonably equivalent value in return. Similarly, various state laws and the U.S. Bankruptcy Code prohibit corporations from preferring some creditors over others. Directors who approve corporate action violating such laws, thereby resulting in harm to the corporation, in turn, may be subject to claims of personal liability for alleged breaches of legal duties.

A corporation may be liable under these laws if it is in financial distress and transfers assets of value without receiving reasonably equivalent value in return.

The laws of many states also provide that directors of financially distressed corporations may be personally liable to the corporation or its creditors for causing the corporation to pay dividends or make other distributions to shareholders. Notably, the current or imminent insolvency of a corporation implicates the directors' duties in a subtle but important manner. Rather than managing the corporation to advance shareholder interests, the directors of an insolvent corporation, and in some states, directors of a corporation in the "zone of insolvency," must seek to maximize the value of the corporation so that the corporation can pay off as many of its legal obligations as possible. The reasoning behind this is straightforward: the corporation's first duty is to meet its legal obligations. When a corporation cannot do that, shareholders' interests become a secondary consideration.

Risk Management, Compliance, and Oversight

Risk management is a particularly salient issue for directors today and a significant part of the directors' duty of oversight of the business and affairs of the corporation. Effective oversight of risk management requires directors to assess the corporation's programs designed to address risks with respect to both strategic and compliance aspects. The board's role is forward-looking, involving overseeing and assessing programs and ensuring that management is implementing programs that effectively manage risk.

Directors should understand and assess the risks confronting the corporation. The board, or an appropriate committee, should require management to provide and should receive periodic reports describing and assessing the corporation's programs for identifying financial, industry, and other business risks and for managing such risks to protect corporate assets and reputation. In addition, the board must ensure that its risk management overview addresses not just legal and compliance issues, but also devotes time to strategy, product innovations, cyclical risks, and the like. Finally, a full understanding of the risk-management controls and infrastructure requires assessing all aspects, including the prevention, mitigation and remediation of risks.

Boards should determine their corporations' risk/reward appetite and risk tolerance in various business areas and oversee those risks effectively. Informed risk-taking is key to achieving the right risk/reward balance. Corporations can and do pursue strategies involving risk—and most worthwhile entrepreneurial activity entails risk. As a result, the board's responsibility with respect to risk is threefold. The board must understand the material risks facing the corporation, including competitive, product, and industry risks. It must also understand the corporation's appetite for risk and ensure that appropriate systems and processes are in place to identify, monitor, and where appropriate, mitigate risk. Finally, it must consider, and sometimes manage, any risks related to governance and compensation that management is unable to manage due to inherent conflicts.

There is no "ideal" risk management program for all corporations. Instead, a board must ensure the corporation's programs address the risks facing their companies in an appropriate manner. The range of risk-management programs is quite broad. Risk management programs may address product liability, quality assurance, information technology security, insurance, legal compliance, plant security, confidentiality, intellectual property, and crisis management. Boards must address core business risks, strategic and competitive risks, and, for example, those associated with product development. Regardless of the industry or risk-management area, the board should have an understanding of the programs more generally, rather than being involved in the day-to-day risk management. To achieve this balance, some corporations designate a chief risk officer and/or create a high-level management committee on risk, either of which reports regularly to the board. Financial services corporations, however, often have board committees focused exclusively on risk. In any case, directors should ensure that they have appropriate information to identify, understand, monitor and evaluate the material risks associated with the corporation and its activities.

Risks typically fall into three general categories: legal, operational, and reputational. Legal risks arise because corporations must comply with laws and regulations, which they sometimes fail to do. Operational risks arise from, for example, strategic failures, inadequate internal controls, corporate governance failures, human or technical error, product innovations or the lack thereof, financial issues, mergers and acquisitions, and external events, such as damage to physical assets from natural or other disasters. Reputational risks arise any time a risk, whether legal or operational, actually occurs. These areas, of course, are interrelated. For example, a failure of a corporation's internal controls can result in a misstatement of revenues, leading, in turn to a restatement, followed by litigation. Thus, an operational risk can lead to a legal risk and, then, to a reputational risk. The remainder of this section develops specific areas of risk management in more detail.

A. Compliance With Law

The board is responsible for overseeing management's activities in assuring the corporation's compliance with legal requirements in the jurisdictions in which the corporation does business. A well-conceived and properly implemented compliance program can significantly reduce the incidence of violations of laws and corporate policy. It can also reduce or eliminate lawsuits, penalties and criminal prosecution. Although the federal sentencing guidelines greatly increase the penalties for corporations guilty of criminal violations, they also provide for significant fine reductions for corporations with effective programs in place to prevent and detect such violations. Directors should periodically satisfy themselves that an appropriate process is in place to detect violations and to encourage not only attention to general legal compliance issues and claims against the corporation, but also the timely reporting of significant legal or other compliance matters to the board or an appropriate board committee.

> *Although the federal sentencing guidelines greatly increase the penalties for corporations guilty of criminal violations, they also provide for significant fine reductions for corporations with effective programs in place to prevent and detect such violations. Directors should periodically satisfy themselves that an appropriate process is in place to detect violations and to encourage not only attention to general legal compliance issues and claims against the corporation, but also the timely reporting of significant legal or other compliance matters to the board or an appropriate board committee.*

Boards should ensure that their companies have formal written policies designed to promote compliance with law and corporate policy. They should review policies periodically for effectiveness, including evaluating the range, depth, and frequency of training and other programs for employees. Further, if the corporation operates in an industry subject to laws and regulations that demand special compliance procedures and monitoring, the review should be more frequent and intensive. Many public companies assign compliance oversight to the audit committee, others to a governance or risk committee. These committees meet regularly with the company's appropriate business operations leaders and general counsel or outside counsel to be briefed on compliance and claims. With the increased burdens placed on public company audit committees, some boards have elected to form a separate compliance or legal affairs committee. Directors should consider whether delegating oversight for multiple compliance issues to a single board committee is sufficient for the corporation's legal and regulatory compliance profile.

The board should ensure that employees of the corporation are informed and periodically reminded of corporate policies, including those pertaining to compliance with (i) codes of business conduct and ethics; (ii) anti-discrimination and employment laws; (iii) environmental and health and safety laws; (iv) anti-bribery laws; (v) antitrust and competition laws; (vi) securities laws, particularly those addressing insider trading; and (vii) laws and regulations of other countries as applicable. The major securities markets require their listed companies to adopt codes of business conduct and ethics applicable to all employees, officers, and directors. The corporation should have appropriate controls throughout the organization for monitoring compliance with such laws and codes. Controls may include whistle blower and hotline policies. The corporation also must establish procedures for addressing violations.

In addition, all compliance personnel should have direct access to the general counsel or other compliance officer to ensure sensitive compliance situations are promptly addressed. In addition, direct reporting access to the board or a board committee can result in "credit" under the U.S. federal sentencing guidelines. Boards should also ensure the compliance program has adequate resources and authority to perform its function.

B. Company Disclosures

The board bears ultimate responsibility for the quality and integrity of company disclosures. Disclosure documents (*e.g.*, annual reports, quarterly reports, current reports, proxy statements, prospectuses, and earnings releases) must fairly present material information about the corporation and its business, financial condition, results, prospects, and risks. Management is responsible for drafting and preparing the corporation's disclosures. Many public companies establish management disclosure committees with responsibility for the company's SEC filings and other public financial disclosures. In other companies, the audit committee handles all financial disclosures. The board should, however, be satisfied that the corporation's procedures for identifying matters requiring disclosure and preparing disclosure documents are reasonably designed to produce accurate and complete public disclosures in an appropriate and timely manner.

> *Directors should be familiar with the corporation's significant filings and be satisfied that disclosures convey all material information about the business in a proper and timely manner.*

In addition to the documents requiring their signatures, directors should be familiar with the corporation's significant filings and be satisfied that disclosures convey all material information about the business in a proper and timely manner.

C. Political Activity

Corporate officers and employees frequently participate in the governmental process on behalf of the corporation by seeking to influence legislative activities, shape regulations, or encourage or prevent government action. Corporations can support or oppose election candidates and engage in political spending. Such actions are often highly visible and can affect the reputation of the corporation and attract shareholder attention. Accordingly, the board should monitor such activities and ensure that they are in accord with regulatory requirements, relevant company policies, and the company's risk profile.

D. Crisis Management

Finally, boards should periodically review whether the corporation has an appropriate crisis management plan in place. It may be appropriate to develop different kinds of crisis management programs and teams to respond to different types of potential emergencies. Board-level monitoring of such programs provides an objective review of management's plans for response, lends credibility to the response, and assures board members are appropriately informed. Such programs include those for natural disasters, significant adverse corporate developments, civil unrest, or terrorist activities. Good crisis management programs address such needs as dissemination of information internally and to the public, provision of back-up systems and records, and adherence to employee safety and business operation procedures during the emergency. A good crisis management plan will also address CEO succession. (See Section 9.F for a more detailed discussion of succession issues.) Members of a crisis management team typically include outside counsel and other advisors.

> *Boards should periodically review whether the corporation has an appropriate crisis management plan in place. It may be appropriate to develop different types of crisis management programs and teams to respond to different kinds of potential emergencies.*

E. Executive Compensation

Compensation can present significant risk management issues and is addressed in Section 8.

F. Other Risks

Boards also oversee other corporate risks. Financial risks can occur in many contexts and require oversight. Asset impairment and acquisition integration situations also present risks for which the board should provide oversight. In addition, employee safety, health and environmental protection, product safety, and human rights are not only matters of legal compliance; they are matters of legitimate public concern with important implications for the long-term success of the corporation. These issues increasingly drive consumer behavior, business partner decisions, employee morale, and business reputation. Compliance with environmental and human rights standards, whether government-mandated or self-imposed, is particularly important. Violations can present public safety and reputation concerns, have a material financial effect and trigger state or federal civil or criminal investigations and liability. For example, global climate change concerns and the advantages of being a "green company" may affect business reputation, culture, morale, and financial performance. The board should periodically engage senior management in discussions of the risks associated with these areas.

Board Structure, Process, and Operations

Board structure, process, and operations significantly affect the board's ability to exercise its powers and discharge its obligations effectively. Properly functioning structures, processes, and operations encourage and reinforce the board's ability to direct the corporation's business and affairs on an informed and objective basis. No model fits every corporation. Instead, each board needs to tailor its approach to the unique

> *Properly functioning structures, processes, and operations encourage and reinforce the board's ability to direct the corporation's business and affairs on an informed and objective basis.*

needs and circumstances of the company. Primary tasks include selecting the chief executive officer, monitoring the performance of the CEO and his or her team, and providing management with advice and counsel.

Boards face a significant challenge in governing effectively given the part-time nature of board service. Most directors have competing demands on their time and attention, and most boards meet on average less often than once a month. Compounding this fact is that the board is comprised of a majority of independent directors who, by definition, have very limited relationships with the corporation outside of their board service. As a result, in addition to time constraints, independent directors have limited information sources about the company other than what management provides. Yet they must form objective viewpoints about the issues facing the company and the quality of the management team to perform fiduciary and other obligations. Careful attention to board structure, processes, and operations helps to overcome time limitations and information asymmetry and otherwise assists the board in establishing a culture and capacity for candor, objectivity, and efficiency.

A. Board Composition

1. Board Size

Each board should determine the appropriate size to accommodate the corporation's needs, objectives, and circumstances. Factors that influence board size include the corporation's need for particular types of expertise on the board, the ability to meet applicable independence or other regulatory standards, the need to populate committees with appropriate expertise as required by regulatory or other board-determined standards, and the need for relationships with significant shareholders or other constituencies. Boards should balance these needs with the fact that a board that is too large can impede effectiveness.

Board size varies substantially among public corporations, with some corporations, like those in the financial services industry, typically having larger boards. Except perhaps for the very largest and most complex corporations, smaller boards (seven to eleven members) generally function more effectively than larger ones, because directors have greater opportunities to participate actively in board deliberations and otherwise contribute. Individuals serving on larger boards may feel that their active engagement is less critical to

> *Except perhaps for the very largest and most complex corporations, smaller boards (seven to eleven members) generally function more effectively than larger ones, because directors have greater opportunities to participate actively in board deliberations and otherwise contribute.*

the functioning of the group. Larger boards can overcome this perception and encourage individual director participation by relying more heavily on board committees in which individual directors actively participate.

2. Qualifications

The board has significant impact on board composition through its powers to nominate and re-nominate directors for election and to fill board vacancies between shareholder meetings. Boards should be prepared to explain why each director is appropriate to the overall board composition and should revisit the "fit" of each director on an annual basis. Boards should make these decisions with an understanding of the company's strategic direction and the board's needs. Indeed, boards should identify the personal qualities required of individual directors (such as integrity, candor, capacity for objective judgment) and identify the overall mix of expertise, experience, independence, and diversity of backgrounds it seeks. The board is more than the sum of its parts, and no one director will have all of the qualifications that the board seeks. The goal is to create a body with the right mix of skill sets, experiences, and diverse viewpoints to contribute to corporate success. The individuals should understand their fiduciary obligations to the company and its shareholders and be capable of expressing objective viewpoints, debating issues, exploring and resolving disagreements, and then—in most instances—forming and supporting a consensus view.

3. Time Commitment

Directors must devote substantial time and attention to their responsibilities, and the time required will vary considerably (depending on the size and complexity of the enterprise and the issues being addressed at a particular time). It is not uncommon for a director's total time commitment to involve 250 hours or more a year, including meeting preparation, travel, meeting attendance, informal consultation with other board members and management, and review of materials to keep up with corporate developments. In addition, directors of the audit and compensation committees have especially significant demands on their time. Certain situations, including change-of-control transactions, financial distress, compliance failures, financial restatements, and management succession crises, also require substantially more time.

Directors considering new or continued board service should consider carefully the time required to meet their responsibilities. Directors should not over-commit themselves, and the nominating/corporate governance committee should consider a board candidate's ability to devote the necessary time before nominating or re-nominating the candidate. Many boards of public companies establish limits on the number of other boards on which directors may serve and also require that directors inform the board before accepting additional board service or other significant commitments.

B. Board Objectivity and Director Independence

Directors must form their own objective judgments about what actions are in the best interests of the company and its shareholders. This obligation extends to assessments of management performance and the strategies and transactions proposed by management. Being an effective guide and sounding board for management also requires objective judgment. Objectivity or "independence of mind" requires constructive skepticism concerning management proposals and reports and the ability and willingness to challenge management constructively and test management's assumptions.

The major securities markets require listed companies (other than controlled companies) to have a majority of "independent" directors. They also require that key oversight committees—audit, compensation, and nominating/corporate governance or any committee to which these committees' duties are delegated—be comprised solely of "independent" directors. In addition, audit committee members must meet the separate definition of audit committee independence set forth in the Sarbanes-Oxley

Act, which is, in some respects, more stringent than the major securities markets' definitions of director independence. The Dodd-Frank Act imposes similar heightened independence standards on compensation committee members.

Generally, the major securities markets provide that a director is independent only if the board makes an affirmative determination that the director is free of any material family, charitable, business, or professional relationship (other than stock ownership and the directorship) with the corporation or its management that is reasonably likely to affect objectivity. When making annual independence determinations, the board should consider all relevant facts and circumstances, and review the materiality of a director's relationships from both the director's standpoint and the standpoint of the individuals or organizations with which the director has an affiliation. Proxy statement requirements call for disclosure of the names of the independent directors, as well as the principles underlying the independence determination and any transactions, relationships, or arrangements that the board considered in the independence determination but were not otherwise disclosed.

The major securities markets identify certain relationships as inconsistent with a finding of independence:

- service by the director as an officer or employee of the corporation or any of its affiliated enterprises (three year look-back);
- receipt by the director of compensation from the company above a threshold amount other than director and committee fees and certain forms of deferred compensation for prior service (three year look-back);
- current business or professional relationships of the director with the corporation or one of its affiliated enterprises above a threshold amount;
- service by an executive officer of the corporation on the compensation committee of a corporation that currently employs the director as an executive officer (three year look-back);
- service by the director as a partner in or an employee of the corporation's external auditor (three year look-back applies

to partners and employees who worked on the company's audit); or

- involvement by a director's immediate family member in one of the foregoing relationships (subject to certain modifications).

Director independence under listing standards does not qualify a director as "disinterested" with respect to any particular board decision. In reviewing director actions in conflict of interest situations or in a special committee context, courts will evaluate the range of business, social, and personal relationships among the directors participating in the decision or transaction and the corporation and its senior managers or other relevant parties.

C. Board Leadership

In many U.S. public companies, the CEO of the corporation also serves as chair of the board. A growing number of public companies have chosen to separate the two functions with the chair position held by an independent director who provides leadership to the board, often serving as a liaison between the board and the CEO, and sometimes serving as a mentor to the CEO. Where the CEO or another non-independent director serves as board chair, the independent directors often formally designate an independent director to act as a presiding or lead director. The chair of the nominating/corporate governance committee or a senior director often acts in that capacity. No one size fits all. Thus, boards need to decide what works best for their company.

The presiding or lead director typically works with the CEO to prepare the board agenda and determine the types of information to be distributed to the board and its committees, presides at executive sessions of the non-management and independent directors, and serves as the board's liaison to the CEO between meetings. The existence of a lead director should not inhibit the ability of individual directors to communicate directly with the CEO. The presiding or lead director may also meet with shareholders or shareholder groups and should promptly inform the full board of such communications. The New York Stock Exchange (NYSE) requires listed companies to identify publicly, by name or position, the director or directors who preside at meetings of non-management directors and to inform shareholders and other interested parties how to communicate with non-management directors. Boards of public companies must disclose their board leadership structure and the rationale for that structure and its relationship to risk oversight.

D. Agenda, Information, and Advisors

Directors should play an active role in setting the board's agenda, ensuring the quality and timely provision of information and access to information, and establishing relationships with key managers and advisors, including, for example, internal auditors, the CFO, and internal and external counsel.

1. Agenda

The board's agenda dictates the matters that come before the board and the focus of board attention. Traditionally, management played a significant role in determining the matters to be presented to and acted on by the board, due to its greater knowledge of the day-to-day operations of the company. For the board to be effective and objective, however, it must control its own agenda. Thus, the trend is toward increasing independent director involvement in determining the board agenda. If there is a non-executive chair of the board or a presiding or lead director, that director and the CEO will often collaborate on the agenda and plans for the meeting. All directors should have the opportunity and feel free to request that an item be included on the agenda. Further, the board should satisfy itself of the overall annual agenda of matters requiring recurring and focused attention, such as the achievement (as well as periodic reexamination and updating) of operational and financial plans, the evaluation of the CEO and other executive management performance, the evaluation of board and committee performance and the adequacy and appropriateness of corporate systems and controls addressing legal compliance, risk management, corporate policy, financial controls, and financial reporting and other disclosures.

2. Information

The quality of the information available to directors significantly affects their effectiveness. Because management is the primary source of information about the corporation, directors should insist that management provide them with information that is (i) timely and relevant, (ii) concise and accurate, (iii) well organized, (iv) supported by any background or historical data necessary to place the information in context, and (v) designed to inform directors of material aspects of the corporation's business, performance, and prospects. Directors should receive agenda-related information sufficiently in advance of board or committee meetings to allow careful study and thoughtful reflection and to accommodate requests for additional information.

The quality of the information available to directors significantly affects their effectiveness.

Many boards also access or receive analysts' reports about the corporation for outside perspective and analysis, as well as benchmarking data. This information allows boards to make comparisons to other corporations in the same industry group or with similar characteristics. Increasingly, directors communicate directly with senior-level employees and managers to learn more about the corporation's business. Some boards schedule site visits for non-management directors so they can directly observe business operations and speak with employees at the operating level of the business.

3. Legal Advisors

Boards generally look to the corporation's general counsel as the primary resource for legal analysis and governance advice.

The general counsel's client is the corporation, as represented by the board of directors, not the CEO or any other officer or group of managers. For this reason, many boards and key board committees meet regularly in a private session with the general counsel. In addition, the board and each of its committees should have access to the corporation's regular outside counsel, if there is one, and should have the authority to retain legal counsel and professional advisors, independent of those who usually advise

Boards generally look to the corporation's general counsel as the primary resource for legal analysis and governance advice. The general counsel's client is the corporation, as represented by the board of directors, not the CEO or any other officer or group of managers.

the corporation. Moreover, the Dodd-Frank Act will require compensation committees to consider conflict of interest factors before engaging legal advisors. A specific circumstance (*e.g.*, allegations of management wrongdoing or negotiating executive pay packages) may prompt the board or, more likely, a board committee to seek independent advice. A board committee may also choose to have regular outside counsel advise the committee generally in meeting its duties and responsibilities.

As part of their annual self-evaluations, the board and each of its committees should consider whether each is receiving appropriate advice as to legal and compliance requirements and timely updates on legal exposure. In addition, each should consider whether it has a good understanding of when to seek legal advice from lawyers other than the general counsel and the outside lawyers regularly engaged by the corporation.

4. Non-legal Advisors

In addition to employees, officers and legal advisors, boards often consult other outside advisors. The need for and degree of consultation varies across companies and industries. For example, boards involved in discussions about a merger or acquisition often engage investment bankers for advice. Although covered in more detail in Section 8, compensation consultants may provide information and expertise in the compensation-setting process. Boards of companies in industries with significant environmental, health, and safety issues may also choose to engage outside consultants to review, for example, environmental safety practices and procedures.

Boards of companies in industries with significant environmental, health, and safety issues may also choose to engage outside consultants to review, for example, environmental safety practices and procedures.

E. Executive Sessions

The major securities markets require periodic meetings of non-management and independent directors in executive session (*i.e.*, without management present) and many public companies hold an executive session every board meeting. These sessions provide a forum for non-management and independent directors to raise issues and ideas they may otherwise be reluctant to raise in the full boardroom, to share candid views about management's performance, to discuss whether board operations are satisfactory, and to raise potentially sensitive issues regarding specific members of management. These sessions are usually coordinated with meetings of the board and, if regularly scheduled, become routine and accepted by management.

If the CEO is also the board chair, most boards designate a director to convene and preside at these sessions. This is a role for a presiding or lead director. Executive sessions may have agendas that are set in advance, but it is also common for the agenda to be open-ended, allowing non-management and independent directors to discuss anything that is on their minds related to the company and its management. Following each session, either the presiding director or the group typically briefs the CEO on what was discussed and on whether any actions are now required.

An executive session should occur during the course of a properly convened board meeting. Directors in an executive session cannot take formal action on behalf of the board when a quorum is not present or if one or more directors have been excluded from the session without consenting to action in their absence. For this reason, and to facilitate open and candid discussions regarding sensitive issues, detailed minutes of executive sessions are not typically kept. It is important, however, to maintain minutes covering attendance and the topics discussed, as well as any recommended actions.

Non-management and independent directors should feel free to meet in executive sessions whenever they feel called to do so and to consider management-sensitive issues, such as controversies involving senior management, change-of-control transactions, or major changes in management. Special advisors, such as special counsel, financial advisors, or others may be appropriate in such cases.

F. Number of Meetings and Scheduling of Meetings

The board should determine its meeting schedule based on an understanding of the tasks to be accomplished over the course of a year and should strive to develop a meeting schedule to optimize the board's time accordingly. The number of meetings a board finds necessary or useful varies with the size, complexity, and culture of the enterprise. Some boards prefer more frequent, shorter meetings, whereas others prefer fewer, lengthier meetings. Some boards schedule one extended planning or strategic meeting each year and shorter meetings during the rest of the year. Boards should hold regularly scheduled meetings at least quarterly, but many schedule six to eight regular meetings a year and hold additional special meetings as needed.

Time at board and committee meetings requires careful scheduling because the length of time budgeted for a meeting limits the topics and depth of the discussion at that meeting. Moreover, meetings should balance management presentations with discussion among directors and with management. Appropriate reports and analyses furnished in advance facilitate discussion at the meeting.

G. Minutes, Note Taking, and Board Materials

All meetings of the board of directors and board committees—whether regular or special meetings or executive sessions—should be memorialized in minutes prepared promptly and circulated for comment and approval. The corporate secretary or another person skilled in preparing minutes should prepare the draft. When the board or committee approves the minutes, the corporation must retain them as a corporate record. Minutes are important legal documents. For example, auditors, courts, regulatory bodies, and shareholders may review them. Therefore, minutes require directors' attention and care.

As appropriate, minutes should contain the following:

(i)   the place, date, and time of the meeting;

(ii)   the attendees (noting who attended in person or by conference call);

(iii)   the chair of the meeting;

(iv)   the topics discussed;

(v)   the matters voted on and the outcome (or a statement of decisions reached by consensus);

(vi)   the directors or other attendees, if any, who abstained from voting or were absent from certain discussions at the meeting;

(vii)   the material terms approved by the board or board committee;

(viii) the materials (incorporated by reference) provided to the directors before and at the meeting;

(ix)   the people who provided information and advice at the meeting;

(x)   the facts surrounding any discussions held or information exchanged between or among some directors before the meeting relating to matters considered at the meeting;

(xi)   the secretary or acting secretary for the meeting; and

(xii)   the time of adjournment.

Although there are differing opinions among corporate advisors about the appropriate level of detail to be included, minutes should be sufficiently detailed to support the availability of the applicable protections provided by substantive law. Thus, minutes should summarize important discussions and actions, without generally purporting to provide a verbatim record or attributing specific words or points of view to particular directors. Minutes that do not reflect that an adequate deliberative process occurred can support an inference that directors failed to consider pertinent information fully and in good faith. Typically, the minutes should reflect appropriately the amount of time devoted to an issue, either by specifically stating the time or by writing the minutes so that the length of the minutes devoted to a particular issue corresponds to the actual time devoted to the issue. The key is to avoid an incorrect inference that less time was devoted to a subject than was in fact the case.

If named as defendants or called as witnesses in litigation, directors will need to explain their actions well after the fact. Detailed minutes provide a contemporaneous record of their deliberative process and can help prevent criticism about the adequacy of that process. Consequently, the minutes should reflect the reality that the directors engaged in a deliberative process, acted in what they reasonably believed to be the corporation's best interests, and considered the possible alternatives.

Note taking implicates similar issues. Directors are not obligated to take notes. Those who do take notes to help them participate should consider whether to retain them. Notes are not subject to a careful process of drafting, review, and approval, and may contain statements or notations that may be misinterpreted, taken out of context, or in fact, be incorrect, particularly if produced in litigation. For example, notes often capture only part of a discussion or fail to distinguish between words spoken and the note taker's thoughts. Similarly, notes and drafts of the secretary of the meeting should normally not be retained after approval of the official minutes.

Furthermore, directors should confirm that the corporation maintains files containing the information provided to the board, such as board books and PowerPoint presentations. This information can help demonstrate the board's informed business judgments and assist directors in recollecting past events. The corporation should develop, with board approval, a consistent policy for the retention of such information so that, together with quality minutes, there is a reliable record of the board's deliberations.

Finally, the corporation's counsel should monitor the consistency of the corporation's approach to minutes and record keeping. With multiple committees and minute takers, inconsistencies in format and approval could arise and create issues in litigation or regulatory proceedings.

H. Board Evaluations

The major securities markets require directors to evaluate, at least annually, the effectiveness of the board and each of its committees. Board and board committee self-evaluations are most effective when planned in advance, with participants having a clear idea of the purpose of the self-evaluation and the issues to be addressed.

Board and board committee self-evaluations are most effective when planned in advance, with participants having a clear idea of the purpose of the self-evaluation and the issues to be addressed.

The typical goal is to consider ways in which the board and its committees can improve their processes. Many boards find director interviews to be a helpful basis for collecting input from individual directors for board and committee discussions. In addition, some boards use written questionnaires to gather information. Questions on these forms must be drafted and used with care. External facilitators may be helpful in collecting information and presenting it in a manner that assures confidential treatment of individual director views. Some boards also use facilitators to lead discussions, providing experience with other companies and an independent perspective. It may be useful to maintain in the minutes a record of the process followed and any specific decisions of the board or committee that resulted, but it is not necessary to retain written materials.

The nominating/corporate governance committee generally conducts or supervises individual director evaluations and is discussed separately in Section 9 of the *Guidebook*.

I. Communications Outside the Boardroom

Directors often have individual communications relating to the corporation with management or with other directors. One-on-one communications can efficiently tap a particular director's expertise or point of view. Indeed, these communications are inevitable.

Excessive communications outside the board and committee rooms, however, particularly between management and a select group of directors, can lead to uneven knowledge among directors about important corporate issues. Such communications may also impair the collective, inclusive, and candid exchange of views at board or

> *Because official action by directors can occur only at a duly called meeting or by unanimous written consent, individual "polling" of directors is not sufficient to authorize action requiring board approval.*

committee meetings and interfere with the board's collegial and independent relationship with management. Moreover, because official action by directors can occur only at a duly called meeting or by unanimous written consent, individual "polling" of directors is not sufficient to authorize action requiring board approval. Instead, the full board or the appropriate committee should discuss issues fully and appropriately at board meetings.

J.   Decision Making

Directors make decisions on a wide variety of matters, sometimes giving direction to management and at other times approving major transactions. Some matters—such as changes in charter documents, authorization of dividends, election of officers, approval of mergers, financings, or corporate liquidations—generally require board action (as well as shareholder action, in some cases) as a matter of law. Directors can take formal action only at duly held meetings of the board or board committee or by unanimous written consent. Unanimous written consents are advisable only for routine matters.

Before taking or approving major actions, directors should receive relevant information to support an informed decision, including summaries and supporting materials. Information is critical to the directors' ability to assess the precise actions proposed. Directors should satisfy themselves with the level of detail they receive and the scope of the resolutions they approve.

> *Before taking or approving major actions, directors should receive relevant information to support an informed decision, including summaries and supporting materials.*

Not all board or committee decisions are formalized by the adoption of resolutions. Some may simply result from a consensus or a "sense of the board" to provide guidance to management. Meeting minutes should adequately describe and memorialize these decisions, and, thereby, avoid any misunderstanding among directors and management.

Business constraints or a crisis can prompt important corporate decisions. A well-developed crisis plan and familiarity with the corporation can enhance decision-making in this context.

K. Disagreements and Resignation

Boards of directors usually make decisions by consensus. Acting in the best interests of the corporation, however, does not require unanimous agreement at all times. If, after a thorough discussion, a director disagrees with any significant action the board is taking, the director should consider abstaining or voting against the proposal. The director should also consider requesting that the abstention or dissent be recorded in the meeting's minutes. Except in unusual circumstances, taking such a position should not cause a director to consider resigning. Resignations should be considered if a director believes that management is not dealing with the directors, the shareholders, or the public in good faith or that the information being disclosed by the corporation is inadequate, incomplete, or incorrect and the director is unable to convince the board to take action. Directors may also consider resigning when they feel their point of view is being disregarded entirely. Public corporations are required to disclose director resignations in an SEC filing, and this disclosure, like others, should be done in consultation with legal advisors.

> *Resignations should be considered in instances where a director believes that management is not dealing with the directors, the shareholders, or the public in good faith or that the information being disclosed by the corporation is inadequate, incomplete, or incorrect, and the director is unable to convince the board to take action.*

Committees of the Board

Committees perform much of the work of the board of directors. No universal mandate exists for a particular committee structure, except for certain actions and duties. In particular, federal law and the major securities markets' listing standards require the audit, compensation, and nominating/corporate governance committees to be composed of independent directors. The boards of some public companies function almost entirely at the board level and delegate to committees only to the extent required. At others, the board acts as a group only on the highest level strategy and policy matters and matters legally required to be addressed by the full board, with most board action and oversight delegated to committees. Each board should tailor its processes and committee structure to the company's specific circumstances, including size, the complexity of its operations and risk management issues, the regulatory schemes applicable to its operations and the competitive environment in which it operates.

Reliance on independent board committees to counterbalance potential conflicts of interest and provide unbiased perspective is intended to improve corporate governance and transparency. Independent directors have become increasingly important in the wake of corporate scandals and market instability. In addition, regulators may require or encourage boards of companies in heavily regulated industries to establish committees to address particular issues. Boards may also delegate to a committee matters that require specialized knowledge or experience or a significant additional time commitment. Unlike the standing committees to which specific responsibilities must be delegated by law or major securities market rules, other board committees may be either permanent committees or specialized committees, which can have a limited duration.

The allocation of specific responsibilities between the full board and its committees, as well as among different committees, varies from company to company. For example, some boards direct their audit committees to handle the primary review and oversight of risk management matters. Other boards assign risk oversight to a specific risk-management committee. Still others retain responsibility for oversight of risk management as a duty of the full board, but delegate certain specialized aspects to the audit, compensation, and governance committees. Some boards create committees devoted to safety or the environment.

Boards may also create special committees to respond to specific circumstances. For example, an allegation of management wrongdoing may prompt a board to form a special committee. Another board, however, might assign the investigation to its audit committee, particularly if the allegations relate to financial, accounting, or internal control issues. In either case, the committee may decide to engage an outside investigation team, particularly if management wrongdoing is implicated.

As this discussion makes clear, statements in this *Guidebook* that particular committees consider certain matters are generalizations. Each board must consider its circumstances and tailor its board structure and allocation of responsibilities accordingly (mindful, of course of applicable SEC and major securities market listing requirements).

Boards should ensure that committees establish appropriate procedures, including keeping minutes and records and providing a regular flow of reports and information to the board to ensure that all directors are kept abreast of each committee's activities and significant decisions.

Directors serving on board committees are subject to the same duties of due care and loyalty and entitled to the same protections of the business judgment rule as they are when acting as members of the full board. Delegation of a given responsibility to a committee does not relieve the full board of ultimate responsibility for oversight of the company. As in other areas of delegation, however, directors may rely upon the efforts of those to whom they delegate if it is reasonable to do so. In accord with their obligation to provide oversight, however, boards should ensure that committees establish appropriate procedures, including keeping minutes and records and providing a regular flow of reports and information to the board to ensure that all directors are kept abreast of each committee's activities and significant decisions.

A. Standing Committees

Some committees are intended to remain in place indefinitely, such as the audit committee, discussed in detail in Section 7, the compensation committee, discussed in detail in Section 8, and the nominating and corporate governance committee, discussed in detail in Section 9. A board may also decide to establish standing committees to oversee ongoing matters, such as risk management or management of complex regulatory schemes. A key factor to consider in creating a standing committee is whether it is more efficient and effective for a smaller group of directors to develop a detailed understanding of the relevant topic and use that expertise to review and monitor the issues within the committee's purview.

Historically, many public company boards appointed standing "executive committees" comprised of directors who were usually officers or who were otherwise available to meet on short notice to address matters between regular meetings of the board. With advances in modern telecommunications, extensive use of executive committees has waned. Indeed, they are often perceived as subordinating the roles of other directors.

B. Special and Other Committees

From time to time, a board may need to create a committee to undertake a specific project or responsibility. In such instances, defining the scope of delegated authority and responsibility of the committee is important. The board should consider and set down in a detailed resolution or committee charter the committee's authority and responsibility. For example, a board may decide to form a special committee of disinterested directors to consider transactions involving conflicts of interest between the corporation and its officers. The members of an *ad hoc* committee need not necessarily meet applicable legal or securities market independence definitions. They should, however, be disinterested in the subject matter and otherwise able to exercise independent judgment. The committee should also establish thorough procedures for its deliberations. A properly constituted and operating special committee will help to reduce the risk of a successful challenge to the board's actions and the potential for director liability.

Public company boards may also form an *ad hoc* committee of independent, disinterested directors to conduct investigations involving potential litigation or wrongdoing. In these cases, the board usually authorizes the committee to engage independent legal counsel and other advisors to help the committee investigate the facts and determine appropriate responses. In each case, the exact scope of authority and functions of the committee will depend upon the unique circumstances of the committee's charge, including the credibility of the allegations, the nature of the alleged wrongdoing and the familiarity of the committee members with the issues. Depending on the scope of authority delegated to the committee, the committee should complete the investigation and then take appropriate action on behalf of the board or recommend an appropriate course of action to the full board of directors.

If allowed under state law, a board may occasionally feel compelled to create a single-person committee. For example, a board may need to react quickly to market conditions and delegate to a one-member committee the authority to price a securities offering. Although single-person committees can be effective in limited contexts, they are not ideal. Multiple directors provide different perspectives on complex issues.

C. Committee Procedures and Activities

Committee composition, procedures, and activities vary from corporation to corporation. The following bullets provide some general guidelines for each area.

- *Committee establishment*—The board should give due consideration to defining the scope of the committee's responsibilities and authority, including:
    - defining the specific issues the committee should address;
    - determining the committee's scope of authority (*e.g.*, is the committee empowered to act on behalf of the board or is the committee to recommend action to the board);
    - ensuring appropriate independence, including the authority to engage independent legal counsel and other advisors at the company's expense;
    - establishing standards for committee operations, including frequency and scheduling of meetings, for example to avoid scheduling conflicts with full board or other committee meetings;
    - ensuring regular reporting to the board;
    - determining whether a committee should be a standing committee or a special committee; and
    - detailing the committee's responsibilities and authority in a written board resolution or in a separate charter approved by the board.
- *Committee composition*—The board should select committee members using criteria appropriate to the committee's purpose and in compliance with any applicable legal and stock exchange requirements. Under most state statutes each member of a board committee must be a duly elected or appointed member of the board of directors. Committee membership criteria may include:
    - experience relevant to committee responsibilities;
    - subject matter expertise that will assist the committee in its work;

- committee members' ability to meet requisite time commitments;
- disinterest in the committee's subject matter; and
- independence from management, as appropriate.

- *Reporting to the board*—Board committees should regularly inform the board of their activities. Generally, standing committees should provide reports at regularly-scheduled full board meetings and circulate to all directors committee agendas, minutes, and written reports, subject to considerations such as the need to protect sensitive information, contractual confidentiality requirements, privacy rights, and governmental security clearance requirements.

- *Legal limits of authority*—Boards and committees must take care to observe applicable limits on their authority. For example, most state corporation statutes require that the board, rather than a committee of the board, approve proposed amendments to the company's articles or certificate of incorporation and similarly require that bylaws (other than those adopted by shareholders) be adopted by the board, rather than by a committee of the board.

- *Scope of delegation and responsibility*—The scope of responsibility of each committee should be tailored to the matters to be addressed. The authority, function, and responsibilities of each committee should be clearly defined. In the past, this was typically done in bylaws or board resolutions. Today, federal statutes and regulations and stock exchange rules require specific duties, responsibilities, and powers to be assigned to specific committees, such as the audit and compensation committees. In addition, the scope of authority and the duties of committees responsible for audit, compensation, and nominating/corporate governance matters must be specified in written charters.

- *Periodic review by the board*—The board or an appropriate committee, such as the nominating and corporate governance committee, should periodically review the responsibilities assigned to each committee and consider whether the assignments of duties and responsibilities continue to be appropriate and consistent with the company's needs and objectives.

Audit Committee

The audit committee is critical to the corporate governance structure, and its existence and some of its functions are legally mandated. It has general oversight responsibility for the company's financial reporting process and internal controls. It also has the exclusive responsibility for retaining and overseeing the performance and independence of the corporation's external auditor. When the external auditor audits the company's internal controls over financial reporting under Section 404 of the Sarbanes-Oxley Act, it will evaluate the committee's performance. The audit committee also increasingly serves as a forum in which the internal and external auditors, as well as the corporation's legal counsel and its compliance and ethics personnel, can candidly report and discuss issues relating to accounting, auditing, financial reporting, risk management, legal, compliance, and ethical matters.

A. Membership

Public company audit committees must consist solely of directors who satisfy the independence requirements of both the company's securities market's listing standards and the federal securities laws. Generally, audit committee members may not receive any compensation from the corporation, such as consulting, advisory or similar fees, other than their director and board committee fees.

The major securities markets require that the audit committee have at least three members. Typically audit committees consist of three to five independent directors. The major securities markets also require that all committee members be financially literate, and at least one audit committee member must have accounting or financial management experience.

In addition, under the Sarbanes-Oxley Act, a public company must disclose in its annual report to the SEC or in its annual meeting proxy statement whether any member of its audit committee qualifies as an "audit committee financial expert," a term defined by SEC regulation and focused on accounting and auditing knowledge and experience. If the committee does not have such an expert, the corporation must disclose why. If the board determines that a committee member qualifies as a "financial expert," the corporation must disclose the name of that member and state whether that expert is independent. Because of this disclosure requirement, most public companies seek to have at least one member of the audit committee qualify as an audit committee financial expert. The requirements for that designation are quite stringent. Thus, directors to be designated as audit committee financial experts should be personally satisfied that they meet those requirements.

Common sense, diligence, and an attitude of constructive skepticism are critical qualifications for an audit committee member. Audit committee members should also have a sufficient understanding of financial reporting and internal control principles to provide oversight for both. New audit committee members should become familiar with key financial issues and accounting practices in the industry or industries in which their corporation operates. All committee members should be current in their knowledge of these financial issues and accounting practices. Continuing education and professional advice, either offered by the corporation or by third party service providers, can be helpful for ensuring members are up to date on best practices and developments.

B. Principal Functions

Federal law, SEC regulations, and securities market listing standards establish many of the audit committee's duties and responsibilities. Audit committees assume other functions as a matter of good practice. Current regulatory requirements for public companies mandate a formal, written charter for the audit committee, specifying the duties and responsibilities. The committee must review the charter annually and publish it on the company's website, or disclose the availability to shareholders, at least once every three years in the corporation's proxy statement.

Audit committee members should understand the tasks in the charter and develop a schedule for performing the tasks. Audit committees generally rely on the corporation's accounting, finance, treasury, internal audit, and legal staffs, as well as the corporation's external auditor, for information. The committee also has the authority to employ its own accountants, attorneys or other advisors, and the Sarbanes-Oxley Act requires the corporation to pay for these advisors. In light of their significant responsibilities, audit committees of public companies often consult with legal counsel to ensure they meet their responsibilities. Identifying the types of information they should receive and review, developing operational procedures and a schedule of tasks, and fulfilling disclosure, accounting, and internal control obligations, are key to audit committee effectiveness. Effective members, of course, also engage in "constructive skepticism."

Audit committee members should understand the tasks in the charter and develop a schedule for performing the tasks. Audit committees generally rely on the corporation's accounting, finance, treasury, internal audit, and legal staffs, as well as the corporation's external auditor, for information. The committee also has the authority to employ its own accountants, attorneys or other advisors, and the Sarbanes-Oxley Act requires the corporation to pay for these advisors.

The following list sets forth the duties for public company audit committees as required by SEC rules and securities markets listing standards. Listing standards vary, so committees should check specific standards.

Audit committees of listed companies are required to:

- select and engage the corporation's external auditor, evaluate the auditor's independence, qualifications and performance, and determine, for each fiscal year, whether to continue that relationship;

- review and approve annually the external auditor's fee arrangements and the proposed terms of its engagement, including the scope and plan of the audit;
- approve, before each engagement, any additional audit-related or non-audit services to be provided by the audit firm, based on the committee's judgment as to whether the firm is an appropriate choice to provide such additional services and whether the engagement might impair the firm's independence;
- establish procedures to receive and respond to any complaints or concerns regarding the corporation's accounting, internal controls, or auditing matters, including procedures for the confidential and anonymous submission by employees of any such complaints or concerns;
- serve as a channel of communication between the external auditor and the board and between the head of internal audit, if any, and the board;
- discuss the corporation's quarterly and annual earnings press releases and financial information and earnings guidance to analysts, the financial press, and rating agencies;
- review the corporation's annual and quarterly financial statements and management certifications, with both management and the external auditor, and discuss with each of them any major issues regarding accounting principles and financial statement presentation and the quality of management's accounting judgments in preparing the financial statements;
- provide oversight of the internal audit function (NYSE-listed companies);
- review the Management's Discussion and Analysis section in each periodic report before filing it with the SEC, and discuss with management and the external auditor any questions or issues that arise in connection with that review;
- review the effect of regulatory and accounting initiatives, as well as off-balance sheet structures, on the financial statements;

- oversee the company's compliance with legal and regulatory requirements;
- set clear hiring policies for employees or former employees of the independent auditors;
- discuss polices with respect to risk assessment and risk management;
- determine whether to recommend to the board that the audited annual financial statements be included in the corporation's annual report on SEC Form 10-K;
- review and approve the audit committee's annual report to shareholders required to be included in a public company's annual meeting proxy statement;
- receive and consider required communications from the external auditor as a result of its timely review of the quarterly financial statements;
- consider, in consultation with the external auditor and the senior internal auditing executive, if any, the adequacy and effectiveness of the corporation's internal controls, which, among other things, must be designed to provide reasonable assurance that the corporation's books and records are accurate, that its assets are safeguarded, and that the publicly reported financial statements prepared by management are presented fairly and in conformity with generally accepted accounting principles;
- review with the external auditor any audit problems or difficulties, and management's response;
- review management's annual assessment of the effectiveness of the corporation's internal controls over financial reporting and the external auditor's audit of internal controls over financial reporting;
- report regularly to the board of directors; and
- conduct an annual self-evaluation.

Other duties and responsibilities that many audit committees undertake as matters of good corporate practice include:

- approve (in coordination with the corporation's nominating or governance committee) any related person transactions between the corporation and its officers or directors, or their family members or enterprises they control;

- establish a direct or "dotted-line" reporting relationship between the internal auditor and the audit committee, with appropriate input in the hiring, compensation, performance review, and the reassignment or firing of the head of internal audit, as well as approving internal audit plans and the budget for the internal audit group;
- consider the appropriate reporting relationship between the chief compliance officer (if other than the chief legal officer) and the audit committee;
- review SEC staff comments on filings;
- review the external auditor's management letter and management's responses to that letter (which generally includes comments on any control deficiencies observed during the audit and other recommendations arising from the audit);
- review primary components of earnings releases prior to public disclosure;
- meet periodically with representatives of the corporation's disclosure committee, if any; and
- if another committee does not do so, meet privately with the corporation's legal counsel or other key advisors to review pending litigation, possible loss contingencies, and other legal concerns, including procedures and policies for addressing legal and compliance issues and reduction of legal risk. (For public companies, this is generally done quarterly in connection with the review of the corporation's Form 10-Q.)

C. Engaging the Auditors and Pre-approving Their Services

One of the key roles of the audit committee is engaging and supervising the company's external auditor. The audit committee reviews and approves the terms of engagement and should know about and understand the scope of the audit. The audit committee must pre-approve all audit and non-audit services the external auditor performs during the year, as well as any audit-related services performed by any other auditing firm. The pre-approval process ensures that the audit committee will consider the effect of any audit and non-audit work on the auditor's independence. In addition, the external auditor must provide an annual letter about its independence to the audit committee of a public company. The committee must discuss this letter with its auditor and consider what effect, if any, non-audit services that the external auditor provides will have on the auditor's independence.

Many audit committees develop policies and procedures to pre-approve specific and detailed types of audit and non-audit services before the need for an engagement arises. Notably, the audit committee must pre-approve all tax services and internal control-related services, engagement by engagement. Some committees delegate this pre-approval authority to the chair (or a subcommittee) of the audit committee to assure that necessary services proceed efficiently, even between audit committee meetings. Any individual or entity that has this authority must report all decisions to the full committee. The audit committee also reviews the hiring of any former personnel of the auditor to assure that it meets regulatory restrictions and will not affect the auditor's independence.

D. Overseeing the Independent Audit

The audit committee is responsible for the appointment, compensation, evaluation and retention of the external auditor. The audit committee should evaluate annually the effectiveness of the external auditor, including verifying the auditor's independence, the auditor's knowledge of the financial issues and accounting standards of the industry or industries in which the corporation operates, and the auditor's effectiveness in providing timely and quality auditing services.

The audit committee should meet with the external auditor during the planning phase of the annual audit to review the plan for the staffing, scope, and cost of the audit and to discuss any areas that may require emphasis or special procedures during the audit. After the audit, the committee should review with the external auditor any problems or difficulties encountered, any significant issues requiring discussion or debate with management during or after the audit, and any letter from the external auditor to management summarizing audit observations together with management's response to that letter. The audit committee should review the findings of the external auditor with respect to any special audit procedures and determine, with advisors' assistance as appropriate, whether revisions to particular corporate policies or procedures are required.

The audit committee should understand significant accounting judgments and estimates that materially affect the corporation's financial statements. Corporations sometimes have a choice among available generally accepted accounting principles or practices. Therefore, the committee should inquire about and understand the effect of alternative choices on reported results. The audit committee should review, at least annually, with the external auditor and with the chief financial officer (CFO) or chief accounting officer (CAO), major issues regarding, and any changes in, choices of accounting principles.

The audit committee should review, at least annually, with the external auditor and with the chief financial officer or chief accounting officer, major issues regarding, and any changes in, choices of accounting principles. Some audit committees find it useful to ask the external auditor to inform the committee what choices the auditor would have made if it, rather than management, had been responsible for preparing the financial statements. The committee also must review with the auditor the quality of management's accounting judgments.

Some audit committees find it useful to ask the external auditor to inform the committee what choices the auditor would have made if it, rather than management, had been responsible for preparing the financial statements. The committee also must review with the auditor the quality of management's accounting judgments.

The audit committee should discuss, often with the participation of the internal auditor, any significant deficiencies or material weaknesses the auditor identified during the course of its annual audit of internal controls. If the auditor identifies any such significant deficiencies or material weaknesses in the company's internal controls over financial reporting, the audit committee should oversee management's timely remediation of those deficiencies. If the audit committee fails to do so, the auditor may conclude that the audit committee constitutes a material weakness in the company's internal controls.

The above-discussed processes and reviews allow the audit committee to determine whether to recommend to the board inclusion of the audited financial statements in the corporation's annual report on SEC Form 10-K. The company's quarterly SEC 10-Q reports may not require a similar process, but many audit committees do review these reports before they are filed.

E. Interaction with Internal Audit

The New York Stock Exchange requires its listed companies to have an internal audit function. The internal auditors typically are employees of the corporation, but some corporations outsource some or all of this function to a firm that is not affiliated with its external auditor.

The audit committee should routinely meet, in private, with the senior internal auditing executive to discuss the external audit function and relationship between the internal and external audit programs, to consider any special problems or issues that may have occurred since the last meeting and to review the implementation of any recommended correc-

The audit committee should routinely meet, in private, with the senior internal auditing executive to discuss the external audit function and relationship between the internal and external audit programs, to consider any special problems or issues that may have occurred since the last meeting and to review the implementation of any recommended corrective actions.

tive actions. The committee should approve the internal audit charter, as well as the annual internal audit plan, before the fiscal year begins. The audit committee should ensure that the internal audit function has sufficient staff resources and budget to fulfill its internal audit plan for the coming year.

If the corporation does not have an internal audit function, the committee should consider with management and the external auditor whether to establish one and, if not, how to obtain the benefits and protections of such a function. If the company has outsourced the internal audit function, the committee should meet regularly with appropriate representatives of that service provider, including meeting in executive session.

F. Meetings with Auditors

Although the CFO or CAO normally attends meetings with external and internal auditors, the audit committee should also meet with the external and internal auditors in executive session, without management present. The NYSE requires its listed companies' audit committees to meet periodically with the external auditor and the head of the internal audit staff, if one exists, separately, in executive session without the participation of other management. These sessions typically cover the following issues, whether (i) the auditors are uncomfortable with any matters regarding the corporation and its financial affairs and records, (ii) the auditors have had any significant disagreements with management, (iii) the auditors have had the full cooperation of management throughout the audit process, (iv) the corporation has reasonably effective accounting systems and controls in place, and (v) the auditor recommends strengthening any material systems or controls or financial staffing. Many audit committees find it useful to have the external auditor describe the two or three issues that involved the most discussion with management during the course of the auditor's work. The committee may also meet with management to discuss the quality of services provided by the external and internal auditors.

The audit committee should discuss with the external auditor and management its role in reviewing quarterly financial reports. They should also discuss the external auditor's procedure for raising significant deficiencies or material weaknesses with the committee or its chair.

As part of the auditor's annual audit of the corporation's internal control over financial reporting, the external auditor must assess whether the audit committee understands and exercises its oversight responsibility over financial reporting and internal controls. As part of this assessment, the external auditor will consider its interaction

The external auditor must assess whether the audit committee understands and exercises its oversight responsibility over financial reporting and internal controls.

with the audit committee, including knowledge about the corporation's accounting policies and internal controls and ability to monitor any control remediation efforts by management. If the auditor concludes that the audit committee's oversight is ineffective, the auditor must report that conclusion, in writing, to the full board.

G. Meeting with Compliance Officers

Unless there is another board committee responsible for compliance, the audit committee should meet as necessary and appropriate, and at least once annually, with the officers responsible for implementing the corporation's codes of business conduct and compliance policies. Officers with compliance responsibilities

The general counsel should meet regularly with the audit committee, or another committee of independent directors, to communicate concerns regarding legal compliance matters, including potential or ongoing material violations of law by the corporation and breaches of fiduciary duties, violation of corporate policies, or ethical violations by senior managers.

typically include the general counsel, chief internal audit officer, and chief compliance officer. These officers should meet with the audit committee outside the presence of other executive officers or directors who are not independent. The responsible officers should also report to the committee periodically. The scope and content of such reports should give the committee timely information about the number and type of concerns reported and investigated, any material violations of law or corporate policies, the sanctions imposed, and any other information to enable the committee to monitor the effectiveness of the overall compliance program. In addition, the general counsel should meet regularly with the audit committee, or another committee of independent directors, to communicate concerns regarding legal compliance matters, including potential or ongoing material violations of law by the corporation and breaches of fiduciary duties, violation of corporate policies, or ethical violations by senior managers.

H. Establishing Procedures to Handle Complaints

The audit committee of a public company must establish procedures, preferably anonymous and confidential, for employees to report concerns or complaints about accounting, internal controls, and auditing matters, as well as violations of the corporation's code of ethics. For global companies, the procedures must comply with the privacy regimes of multiple countries. Audit committee members are not usually in the best position to conduct fact-finding or even to receive complaints or concerns in the first instance. Instead, the committee should create, with management's assistance, procedures adequate to ensure that information reaches the committee in a form conducive to identifying "red flags" and to ensuring timely and efficient committee review and resolution of any issues. For example, the audit committee may decide to rely on an ethics or compliance officer to gather, review, and process information, or it may decide to outsource this task to a third-party service provider.

In addition, lawyers for public companies (both internal and outside counsel) may be required to report to a committee of independent directors, or to the board, credible evidence that a material violation of securities laws, breach of fiduciary duty, or similar violation by the issuer or any of its officers, directors, employees, or agents has occurred, is occurring, or is about to occur. Public companies may determine that the audit committee is the appropriate committee to receive such reports. If so, the audit committee should have a process for acting on reports, including an understanding about arranging for legal advice from outside counsel when appropriate.

I. Meetings and Compensation

The audit committee should discuss and determine the number of meetings it needs to hold annually in order to deal effectively with its responsibilities. The major securities markets' listing standards require audit committees to review quarterly and annual reports filed with the SEC, and as a result, the audit committee should meet at least four times a year. It is common for public company audit committees to have an in-person or telephonic meeting with the company's CEO, CFO, other senior financial managers, and external auditor in advance of each quarterly or annual earnings release. As a result, almost all audit committees schedule at least four, and some as many as five to eight, meetings per year.

It is important that the schedule for board and other committee meetings and activities not unduly limit the time for audit committee deliberations. Membership on the audit committee requires a significant commitment of time. Committee meetings are often several hours in length, and some extend for an entire day. As a result, some boards provide the audit committee members with a higher level of compensation, often through meeting fees. Others have determined that differential compensation among board committee members can create the risk of divisions within the board and may make selection of members and rotation of committee assignments more difficult. Nonetheless it is important that audit committee members be compensated adequately for the time and effort they devote to the corporation to fulfill their fiduciary and technical responsibilities as committee members.

Compensation Committee

Executive compensation plays a central role in attracting, retaining and motivating the management talent critical to the corporation's success. The compensation committee is responsible for approving executive compensation and, in many cases, for overseeing the planning for management succession. The integrity and transparency of the committee's decision-making process are of paramount concern to shareholders and regulators alike. Real abuses and perceived excesses in executive compensation policies, plans, and programs at some notable public companies led to many of the federal corporate governance reforms related to compensation. For example, investors' desire for greater transparency in executive compensation in general, and compensation committee decision-making in particular, resulted in the SEC's complete overhaul of the proxy disclosure requirements for executive compensation in 2006 and 2009, as well as specific requirements in the Dodd-Frank Act in 2010.

The legislative and regulatory, as well as public, scrutiny of the role of executive compensation in connection with (and as a contributing factor to) the recent global financial downturn suggests that shareholder and regulatory interest in executive compensation is not likely to wane. Regulators are now working on rules implementing the executive compensation and corporate governance provisions of the Dodd-Frank Act, which include mandatory say-on-pay votes for all public companies, as well as additional executive compensation disclosures relating to the relationship between the CEO's total pay and the company's median employee's total pay, and the relationship between executive compensation and the company's financial performance.

These recent executive compensation and corporate governance reforms reflect Congress's heightened focus on the role of the compensation committee as the primary corporate decision maker for compensation matters. In performing this function, the compensation committee should consider the following questions:

- How should compensation packages for the CEO and other senior executives be determined, including (i) who should do the negotiating; (ii) what are the relevant companies, and/or peer companies, with which to compare the corporation's compensation packages; and (iii) what is the appropriate role, if any, for compensation consultants and other advisors in setting compensation levels and elements?
- Is management's compensation reasonably related to personal and corporate performance, and does it appropriately motivate management to build value for shareholders?
- Do compensation programs and policies focus management incentives on the appropriate time horizons, or do they encourage inappropriate or excessive short-term risk taking?
- Over time, are the compensation programs and policies attracting and retaining quality management for the corporation?
- Do a corporation's public disclosures about executive compensation give shareholders an accurate picture of senior executive compensation and the reasoning behind executive compensation decisions?
- Under what circumstances should the corporation recover previously awarded compensation, and how should the corporation's compensation "clawback" policy function, given legislative and regulatory requirements, including (i) which officers and employees will be subject to the policy, (ii) what types and amounts of compensation are subject to potential recovery, and (iii) how should the policy be implemented to ensure enforceability?
- Are severance, change-of-control, and post-employment benefits properly related to corporate interests and reasonable in amount?

The compensation committee should apply independent judgment to determine the compensation arrangements and levels that are in the best interests of the corporation. When functioning effectively, the compensation committee provides credibility and substance to the concept of independent oversight of executive compensation.

> *The compensation committee should apply independent judgment to determine the compensation arrangements and levels that are in the best interests of the corporation. When functioning effectively, the compensation committee provides credibility and substance to the concept of independent oversight of executive compensation.*

A. Membership

The compensation committee should, and generally must, consist solely of independent directors. The Dodd-Frank Act will require the major securities markets to revise their listing standards to require that compensation committee members satisfy heightened independence standards. In addition, under the federal tax laws, decisions of most public companies to pay certain highly compensated executives more than $1 million annually must be made by directors who meet the Internal Revenue Service's definition of "outside director" in order for the compensation to qualify for a full federal tax deduction. Moreover, SEC rules exempt executive officer option grants from profit recapture only if "non-employee directors," as defined in those rules, make the grant decisions. Each of these terms is similar to, but not the same as, the "independent director" definitions in stock exchange listing standards. Consequently, the eligibility of prospective compensation committee members should be reviewed against each standard. Interlocking compensation committee memberships are strongly discouraged, trigger additional proxy statement disclosures, and may disqualify a director from "independent" status under listing standards. For example, if an executive officer of a corporation serves on the compensation committee of another company, and an executive officer of that other company serves on the first corporation's compensation committee, they are considered to be "interlocking."

Apart from legal considerations, the compensation committee's independence from management gives greater credibility to the compensation committee's key responsibility: to establish and approve compensation for executive officers on behalf of the corporation. Further, even when a director meets the independence requirements of the applicable listing standards, close personal or business ties between the director and the CEO may mean, or at least create the appearance, that the director is not an appropriate member of the compensation committee. As with board membership generally, diverse backgrounds, expertise, and experiences can provide useful perspectives in compensation committee deliberations.

B. Principal Functions

The principal functions of the compensation committee are to:

- oversee the corporation's overall compensation structure, philosophy, policies, and programs and assess whether they establish appropriate incentives for senior executives;
- review and approve corporate goals and objectives relevant to the CEO and senior executive compensation and annually evaluate executive performance in light of those goals and objectives;
- establish the compensation and benefits of the CEO and executive officers;
- assess how compensation policies and programs contribute to or affect the company's risk profile and structure them to create incentives for management to make risk-appropriate decisions;
- evaluate and approve employment agreements with executive officers;

- establish and periodically review policies for the administration of executive compensation programs (including all equity-based plans and perquisites);
- make recommendations to the board with respect to incentive compensation plans and equity-based plans generally;
- review and be satisfied with the corporation's Compensation Discussion and Analysis disclosure and discuss with management any issues or questions arising from that review;
- review and approve the annual report of the compensation committee for inclusion in the annual meeting proxy statement; and
- conduct an annual self-evaluation.

1. Decision-Making Process

The compensation committee independence requirement is designed to promote objective judgment on the sensitive matter of management's compensation, and in particular, the compensation of the CEO. At a minimum, the compensation committee should create a thorough process to reach an informed decision that is something more than rubber-stamping somebody else's recommendations. How much more, of course, depends on the compensation committee's judgment, as well as the facts and circumstances of the situation.

The compensation committee should create a thorough process to reach an informed decision that is something more than rubber-stamping somebody else's recommendations. How much more, of course, depends on the compensation committee's judgment, as well as the facts and circumstances of the situation.

A compensation committee should consider the most effective process for reaching an independent and informed decision about the appropriateness of the amount and composition of management's compensation packages. The compensation committee may benefit from engaging and collaborating with competent, experienced, and independent compensation consultants, who can assist in collecting comparative data and advise on the best compensation packages for the corporation. Indeed, the Dodd-Frank Act authorizes compensation committees to retain and oversee independent advisors. Regardless of whether the committee engages outside consultants or counsel for assistance, the committee is ultimately responsible for approving the terms, amounts and forms of compensation.

Utilizing the resources of advisors, particularly those engaged by the compensation committee and independent of the company and senior management, can give credibility and substance to the independent oversight of executive compensation. The type of advisors and the extent of their use can vary depending on each executive's position within the company and on a variety of other facts and circumstances. For example, an outside CEO brought in to lead the company may warrant a different process than the lifelong insider of many years. In addition, if an executive engages his or her own lawyer to negotiate the terms of the employment agreement, the compensation committee should consider how best to protect the corporation's interest in the process—for example, engaging its own or company counsel to help negotiate the agreement.

> *Utilizing the resources of advisors, particularly those engaged by the compensation committee and independent of the company and senior management, can give credibility and substance to the independent oversight of executive compensation.*

Management's participation in the compensation committee's decision-making process is a particularly sensitive area. Although a company's CEO will often meet with the compensation committee, she or he should not be present during most of its deliberations and should never be present during deliberations regarding his or her own compensation. The same is true of the corporation's general counsel and senior compensation or human resources executive. Both the reality and the appearance of independent oversight are important; therefore, it is wise to have compensation committee discussions on executive compensation matters occur without members of management present.

The committee should consider the CEO's compensation in a private session, without the CEO or the CEO's subordinate officers.

With respect to compensation policies and decisions for non-employee members of the corporation's board of directors, the best practice is for the entire board to make or approve the policies and decisions, rather than just the compensation committee.

2. Structure and Components of Executive Compensation

The basic principle that a significant portion of an executive's compensation should be tied to the corporation's strategic objectives and financial performance, with an appropriate balance between short- and long-term incentives, should guide the compensation committee. The structure and components of an executive compensation package vary among industries and companies. Benchmarking against peer companies is sometimes used as a tool to help determine executive compensation, but the committee

> *The basic principle that a significant portion of an executive's compensation should be tied to the corporation's strategic objectives and financial performance, with an appropriate balance between short- and long-term incentives, should guide the compensation committee.*

should avoid simply matching or exceeding the compensation structure of peer companies. In addition, peer companies should be selected carefully, with company size, financial condition, industry characteristics, competitive factors, location, and corporate culture as relevant factors. Many companies have compensation consultants prepare summaries focused on the regions in which the companies compete for talent, the industries within which they principally work, and their market capitalization. Some companies may also use more than one peer group for executives, if the markets for which the companies compete for executive talent differ for one or more positions.

Compensation committees have a wide variety of tools for equity incentives, such as restricted stock, restricted stock units, stock appreciation rights, stock options, and other types of equity compensation. Although historically stock options were commonly used because there was no charge to earnings associated with the grant of "at the market" stock options, current accounting rules now require companies to recognize a non-cash expense in connection with all stock options, thereby eliminating the accounting benefit of granting options as compared to other forms of equity compensation. In addition, overhang strains and the economic downturn in late 2008 left many previously granted options under water and considerably weakened the existing incentives. Consequently, some compensation committees have begun to grant other forms of equity compensation, such as restricted stock or restricted stock units, or awards that vest to a greater extent in later years or vest only when recipients meet specified performance goals. In choosing the form and vesting schedule and conditions of an award, compensation committees should carefully consider whether the award provides the intended incentive, for example, by taking into account other awards already held, including the exercise prices and vesting of such awards, the accounting expense of the award, the tax effect of the award both for the company and the individual, and the administrative complexity of the award.

Compensation committees also often require retention or holding periods for stock, whether granted or obtained on option exercise. This can help to align executive pay more effectively with long-term performance. Many companies also establish stock ownership targets to further align the executives' interests with those of shareholders. Some companies prohibit activities that attempt to hedge against a decrease in the value of the company's equity securities. The Dodd-Frank Act requires that companies disclose whether employees or directors may engage in hedging transactions.

The compensation committee should also review the benefits and perquisites provided to senior executives, particularly when approving employment contracts. "Perks" have received considerable attention due to perceived excesses in their use, such as personal use of corporate aircraft, tax gross-ups, and use of company resources post-employment. As a result, the SEC requires enhanced disclosure of perks. Another important area of scrutiny is retirement, termination, and change-in-control benefits. There is widespread shareholder concern that these benefits are not sufficiently related to job performance, and compensation committees should be aware that these benefits could be viewed as excessive even when fully disclosed in the annual Compensation Discussion and Analysis. For example, some institutional investor groups now recommend that constituents withhold votes from, or even vote against, members of the compensation committee or board of directors that approve a new or materially modified employment agreement that includes a tax gross-up.

In addition, committee members should understand the interplay of all compensation arrangements—fixed, incentive, benefits, perquisites, deferred compensation, retirement, severance, and change in control—so that unintended or disproportionate benefits do not accrue to the senior executive. To facilitate this understanding, at many public corporations senior management or independent compensation consultants annually provide committee members with a clear and comprehensive presentation detailing all elements and amounts of compensation paid to each senior executive, as well as the value of potential retirement, severance, and change in control

> *Committee members should understand the interplay of all compensation arrangements — fixed, incentive, benefits, perquisites, deferred compensation, retirement, severance, and change in control — so that unintended or disproportionate benefits do not accrue to the senior executive.*

benefits to which the executive could become entitled (sometimes referred to as a "tally sheet"). The SEC's 2006 compensation disclosure rules increased the need for an accurate computation of these amounts. These rules require public corporations to disclose details about the dollar value of all elements of executive compensation, as well as estimates of benefits that could become payable to senior executives either upon a termination of employment or upon a change in control of the corporation.

The compensation committee also has a role in risk oversight for company compensation policies and practices. Under the 2009 SEC executive compensation rules, companies must analyze their compensation policies and practices and disclose whether those policies and practices encourage excessive risk taking and are reasonably likely to have a material adverse effect on the company. In most companies, management, in some cases working with compensation consultants, prepares this analysis and makes the initial determination regarding the companies' policies and practices by tallying all of the elements of compensation, determining the risks posed by each element, and then analyzing any mitigating factors. The compensation committee, however, retains an oversight role, and management should detail its procedures for committee approval and provide the committee with a summary of its analysis and determination. In some cases, the compensation committee may want to take a more active role in risk oversight for compensation policies and practices by reviewing and approving management's comprehensive analysis or even conducting its own analysis with input from its compensation consultants.

The proper design of a compensation program is just the starting point. The program requires at least annual performance evaluations of the participating executives against pre-established performance targets (which may include comparison against the performance of peer corporations), as well as ongoing review of the program's effectiveness. The compensation committee should keep the board informed of the results of these periodic reviews.

3. Documentation of Approval of Executive Compensation

The compensation committee should review with senior management the corporation's procedures for accurately and timely documenting the grants or issuances of equity awards, both in the compensation committee's minutes (or other written action) and in the documentation evidencing the awards. Detailed compensation committee minutes or resolutions that adequately discuss the compensation committee's rationale, deliberation, and consideration regarding the grants or issuances of equity awards and any other form of executive compensation, are considered best practices and can assist the corporation in the preparation of its annual Compensation Discussion and Analysis. As a general matter, a corporation should have adequate written procedures relating to the grants or issuances of equity awards, including the timing and pricing of such grants or issuances, to help protect the corporation, its executives, and the compensation committee against claims of manipulation or abuse in the timing or pricing of such grants or issuances of equity awards. Best practices also include granting equity awards at pre-scheduled meetings that fall outside of company blackout periods for employee trading of company securities and avoiding the use of actions by written consent and delegation to officers.

4. Legal Restrictions on Executive Compensation

The compensation committee should become familiar with and receive legal advice as to legal restrictions on compensation to officers and directors, whether under a shareholder approved plan or otherwise. The Sarbanes-Oxley Act prohibits most personal loans and extensions or arrangements of credit from a public company to its directors and executive officers. In addition, the Dodd-Frank Act requires that companies adopt a "clawback"

> *The compensation committee should become familiar with and receive legal advice as to legal restrictions on compensation to officers and directors, whether under a shareholder approved plan or otherwise.*

provision, applicable in the event of a restatement of financial statements, providing for recovery of excess amounts of any bonus or other incentive- or equity-based compensation received during the 3-year period preceding the restatement. The clawback provision must cover all current and former executives.

Regardless of the requirements of the federal securities and other laws, in circumstances in which there has been a restatement indicating that the bases on which incentive-based compensation has been paid are no longer correct, the compensation committee or other independent directors should consider whether to recover any compensation on the basis of unjust enrichment. In addition, if the restatement resulted from employee misconduct, the compensation committee or other independent directors should consider whether to take action to discipline or dismiss, as well as to recover compensation paid to, any employee involved in the misconduct.

To assist with the recovery of such compensation, and in light of mandatory clawback provisions, the compensation committee should consider incorporating clawback provisions into the terms of incentive compensation programs or arrangements. For example, the provisions could, in certain circumstances, contractually obligate the employee to return any such compensation to the corporation. In particular, and in light of recent legislation, the compensation committee should determine the circumstances under which the corporation would be entitled to clawback, including determining the eligible employees and types and amounts of compensation to be subject to the policy, as well as determining how to implement the policy, accounting for enforceability factors. The compensation committee should consider the potential effect of compensation provisions on its ability to attract and retain executives and on investor and shareholder concerns regarding the corporation's executive compensation programs and arrangements.

C. Disclosure of Compensation Decisions

Public company managers must prepare a section of the annual meeting proxy statement called Compensation Discussion and Analysis, which is a detailed discussion of the key elements of the corporation's executive compensation policies and decisions. This disclosure discusses the principles underlying executive compensation decisions and should include a discussion

> *Public company managers must prepare a section of the annual meeting proxy statement called Compensation Discussion and Analysis, which is a detailed discussion of the key elements of the corporation's executive compensation policies and decisions.*

regarding the rationale behind the adoption of such principles and explain executive compensation decisions in light of the principles. The Dodd-Frank Act requires a non-binding shareholder vote, at least once every three years, to approve compensation of named executive officers. This vote will take place at annual or other shareholder meetings for which the SEC requires disclosure. In addition to this say-on-pay vote, the legislation also requires a non-binding vote every six years to determine the frequency of say-on-pay votes.

The Compensation Discussion and Analysis must include a discussion of the following:

- the objectives of the corporation's compensation programs;
- the results the compensation program is designed to reward;
- the elements of compensation;
- the reasons the corporation chose to pay each element;
- the manner in which the corporation determines the amount (and the formula, if any) for each element of pay; and
- the way each compensation element and the corporation's decisions regarding that element fit into the corporation's overall compensation objectives and affect decisions regarding other compensation elements.

The compensation committee should scrutinize closely the corporation's policies and procedures relating to the disclosure of executive officer compensation. Consultation with external compensation specialists may be necessary to assist the committee in formulating the Compensation Discussion and Analysis. Because the committee makes many decisions for senior executives outside the presence of management, the committee should assist management in its preparation of the Compensation Discussion and Analysis (for example, by providing detailed minutes that reflect and highlight the various factors it weighed and considered) and then review and be satisfied with the disclosure's accuracy. The compensation committee must also state, in a separate report in the proxy statement, that its members have reviewed and discussed the Compensation Discussion and

Analysis with management and, based on this review and discussion, recommended that it be included in the proxy statement.

The compensation committee should also work with management and review management's analysis and assessment of whether compensation policies and practices create risks that are reasonably likely to have a material adverse effect on the company. The compensation committee should seek appropriate assurances from management and legal counsel that all disclosures required by law and by the applicable national stock exchange listing standards are being made, and that rules related to shareholder approval of equity compensation plans and the reporting of grants of and trades in the corporation's securities are being observed. The compensation committee, along with counsel, should discuss and consider how to document adequately the process leading to the compensation disclosures in a manner that supports the disclosures made.

In addition, the Dodd-Frank Act requires companies, depending on their status, to make specific disclosures, including:

- indicating whether the committee retained a consultant and its consideration of the factors for doing so (listed companies, but controlled companies exempt);
- indicating whether the committee's work has raised any conflicts of interest, and if so, how they were resolved (listed companies, but controlled companies exempt);
- demonstrating the relationship between executive compensation and financial performance (public companies);
- stating the ratio between the CEO's compensation and the median compensation of all other employees (public companies); and
- indicating whether, as discussed above, certain hedging transactions are permitted (public companies).

The SEC will promulgate further regulations in this area, including specific regulations for financial institutions, and the national securities markets are required to issue related listing rules.

D. Independent Advice for the Compensation Committee

The Dodd-Frank Act requires that committees have the power to hire (without management influence in the selection process) compensation specialists, consulting firms or other experts to assist in the evaluation of executive officers and the development of a compensation program so that it need not rely solely upon management-selected corporate personnel or outside specialists for advice and guidance.

Given increased public scrutiny and the most recent executive compensation and corporate governance reforms, including those in the Dodd-Frank Act, relating to the need for compensation committees to obtain advice from independent advisors, the committee should consider the following types of factors prior to engaging an advisor: (i) the other services performed by the advisor for the corporation, (ii) the amount of fees paid to the advisor for such services, and (iii) the existing personal and business relationships between the advisor and the corporation, including with management. At all times following the engagement, the compensation committee should be made aware of any new relationships that develop between the advisor and the corporation or management.

The compensation committee's need for independent advice is particularly critical when the compensation committee exercises its obligations with respect to reviewing and approving employment, retention, change-in-control and/or severance agreements with executives. As a result, for example, the Dodd-Frank Act requires the compensation committee to have full authority, stated in its charter, to approve its advisors' fees and other terms of engagement and should make clear that the advisors work for

> *The compensation committee's need for independent advice is particularly critical when the compensation committee exercises its obligations with respect to reviewing and approving employment, retention, change-in-control and/or severance agreements with executives.*

the compensation committee, not management. Compensation consultant fees and other services by the consultant must be publicly disclosed in certain circumstances. The advisor should have direct access to the compensation committee, without the presence of management, to help preserve the advisor's independence. Outside advisors should also have direct access to senior executives in order to obtain information necessary to provide the compensation committee with independent advice.

E. Other Responsibilities

Other responsibilities that the compensation committee may undertake include reviewing and monitoring the effectiveness of employee pension, profit sharing, 401(k), and other benefit plans and programs, taking into account the importance of retaining, motivating, and incentivizing the employees of the corporation, as well as the overall cost to the corporation of such programs. Compensation committees should carefully consider whether they are or should be fiduciaries with respect to the corporation's pension, 401(k), or other employee benefit plans that are subject to regulation under the Employee Retirement Income Security Act (ERISA). Under ERISA, plan fiduciaries are subject to heightened scrutiny and responsibility with respect to the investment of plan assets. The compensation committee has a duty to be informed about the corporation's compensation and benefit structure; however, most compensation committees do not act as fiduciaries for ERISA-covered benefit plans. Directors and

Other responsibilities that the compensation committee may undertake include reviewing and monitoring the effectiveness of employee pension, profit sharing, 401(k), and other benefit plans and programs, taking into account the importance of retaining, motivating, and incentivizing the employees of the corporation, as well as the overall cost to the corporation of such programs.

high-level executives typically are privy to non-public information regarding the corporation's performance and finances. As a result, they can be in the difficult position of having to choose between their duties as officers or directors under state and federal laws to keep such information confidential, and their duties as plan fiduciaries possibly to disclose or act upon such information for the benefit of plan participants. Often, rather than having directors or senior officers designated as plan fiduciaries, corporation employees (but not the most senior executives) will serve as the fiduciaries of the corporation's ERISA-covered benefit plans. Increasingly, however, corporations are engaging independent fiduciaries to make some or all of the investment decisions for their ERISA-covered benefit plans. This separation can help insulate the corporation from potential conflicts of interest related to such investment decisions, particularly with respect to any decisions to invest plan assets in the stock of the corporation.

Nominating and Governance Committee

An effective nominating and corporate governance function is critical to board performance. This committee's stature and importance has increased with the growth in company size, investor focus on board composition and performance, and the financial crisis. It also has transformed into a corporate governance committee or a nominating and governance committee.

Major securities markets' listing standards prescribe some elements of the nominating and corporate governance function. Generally, the committee is responsible for recruiting and maintaining board members with the appropriate skills and independence for quality decision-making. It also implements and oversees the operation of corporate governance principles for both board process and the corporation's business.

A. Membership

The nominating and governance committee should be composed solely of independent directors. The NYSE requires that each of its listed companies has a committee composed entirely of independent directors, with a written charter that addresses the committee's process to identify individuals qualified to become directors, to select, or to recommend that the board select, director nominees, and to develop and recommend to the board a set of corporate governance principles for the corporation. NASDAQ rules do not mandate a nominating or corporate governance committee but do require that either a committee of independent directors (subject to limited exceptions) or a majority of independent board members select or recommend director nominees. As a practical matter, because SEC rules require public disclosure of reasons for a corporation's lack of a nominating committee, virtually all NASDAQ companies maintain such a committee.

B. Criteria for Board Membership

A nominating and governance committee should establish, or recommend to the board, criteria for identifying appropriate director candidates. These criteria are usually in governance principles or a separate policy. The committee should lead the recruitment and selection process. The attributes of an effective corporate director include strength of character, an inquiring and independent mind, practical wisdom, and mature judgment. In addition to these personal qualities, the committee may want to emphasize individual qualifications such as diversity, technical skills, career specialization, specific industry experience, or expertise in matters such as compensation or governance. The effective nominating committee seeks director attributes to complement and expand the attributes of the existing board members. Of course, the committee must address certain requirements, such as identifying a director who qualifies as an "audit committee financial expert" for

The attributes of an effective corporate director include strength of character, an inquiring and independent mind, practical wisdom, and mature judgment. In addition to these personal qualities, the committee may want to emphasize individual qualifications such as diversity, technical skills, career specialization, specific industry experience, or expertise in matters such as compensation or governance. The effective nominating committee seeks director attributes to complement and expand the attributes of the existing board members.

accounting and financial reporting purposes, or explain why it does not have such an expert. Public companies are also emphasizing diversity considerations in their desired board profile, recognizing that diversity can contribute significant value by providing additional perspectives to board deliberations. The articles or certificate of incorporation, bylaws, or board policies may include other qualifications for directors, such as age or length of service limitations or relevant experience.

There is no one-size-fits-all approach to director searches. The desired outcome is a board that can build consensus and effectively exercise collaborative judgment. Some boards also look for specific skills and experiences to build on what they currently possess, lack, or need to strengthen. This type of focus can help direct the search toward candidates who can provide needed additional talent and experience to the corporation.

Most corporate governance commentators recommend that a board of a public company have a substantial majority of independent directors, and the major securities markets require at least a majority of independent directors. When considering director independence, the committee should also bear in mind broader judicial standards of disinterestedness applicable for judicial review of conflict of interest or other issues. As a result, the committee should evaluate the full range of business and personal relationships between director candidates and the corporation and its senior managers.

Although independent directors are essential to a well functioning board, the board must be able to receive candid input from senior management. In addition to input from the CEO, who is typically on the board, the committee should consider how best to have access to senior management to ensure that input. Some nominating and governance committees determine that senior officers, in addition to the CEO, should serve as directors, whereas others decide that attendance at board or committee meetings by senior officers in a non-director capacity is sufficient to facilitate the board's ready access to information regarding the business and operations of the corporation. Although it is not typical to have senior executives, beyond the CEO, on the board, in an appropriate case, their presence can serve to enhance succession planning and facilitate a peer relationship and firsthand contact.

C. Evaluating Board Incumbents

The nominating and governance committee is also responsible for evaluating incumbent directors. The committee should thoughtfully consider each director's contribution and the needs of the board before deciding whether to recommend renomination. This is a good practice and can help address the common criticism that election or appointment to the board is tantamount to tenure. It is also responsive to SEC disclosure rules requiring disclosure of director qualifications justifying service. The committee should consider attendance, preparation, participation, and other relevant factors. Tools to assist in the evaluation process may include confidential discussions led by the board chair, lead director, or corporate governance committee chair, self-evaluations, and peer evaluations. Outside consultants can also be effective in the evaluation process.

Boards handle the sensitive issue of board succession, including underperforming directors, in a variety of ways. Many boards attempt to deal with the issue indirectly through the adoption of mandatory retirement policies, but these policies can create an expectation that board service continues until retirement. In fact, a well-functioning nominating committee should be able to decline to nominate incumbents for reelection as individual situations dictate.

D. Nominating Directors

The nominating and governance committee approves and selects, or recommends that the board select, director nominees, including both incumbent directors and new candidates. The committee also recommends candidates to the board to fill interim director vacancies.

The committee should encourage all directors, including management directors, to suggest candidates for the board. The committee should also seek out candidates and can employ search consultants to assist in identifying appropriate candidates. The committee's charter should give the committee the authority to retain a search firm to identify director candidates, including the authority to approve the search firm's fees and other retention terms. The committee should control the process, including making decisions with respect to nominees and recommending to the full board a slate of nominees. Moreover, the committee should be the conduit for communication regarding shareholder recommendations for director nominees.

The board's comprehensive plan for shareholder communications may encourage the committee to seek suggestions for director candidates from its institutional investors and other shareholders.

The board's comprehensive plan for shareholder communications may encourage the committee to seek suggestions for director candidates from its institutional investors and other shareholders. Both the non-executive chair, if there is one, or a lead or presiding director and the nominating/corporate governance committee chair should be prominently involved in the recruiting process in order to ensure that the committee is making nominating decisions and not the CEO or other insiders.

Public company proxy statements must disclose the nominating and governance committee's procedures and policies for considering director candidates, as well as the particular experience, attributes, skills, and qualifications the committee focused on in selecting or recommending each director candidate. Indeed, the proxy statement affords a board the opportunity to explain why it believes a nomination is warranted. Furthermore, public companies must disclose whether, and if so, how, the nominating and governance committee considers diversity in identifying director nominees. If the nominating/corporate governance committee has a diversity policy, the company must disclose how the policy is applied and how the committee assesses the policy's effectiveness. The purpose of these disclosure requirements is to increase shareholder understanding of the nominating process. Accordingly, the committee should review its procedures and policies to ensure that they are consistent with the committee's circumstances and operations and that they are sufficiently formalized to provide that understanding and to satisfy the scrutiny of public disclosure.

E. Recommending Committee Members and Chairs

In addition to nominating directors, the nominating and governance committee will often make recommendations to the board regarding the responsibilities and organization of all board committees. The committee should also recommend qualifications for membership on committees. The committee may also make annual recommendations of specific individuals for membership on standing committees. Although some boards have a policy of periodic rotation of committee memberships among the directors to develop expertise and allocate equitably the time commitment, rotation may be more difficult for the audit committee than for others. The committee should also address the process for board decision-making regarding the appointment of and changes in the chair and members of each board committee.

F. Chief Executive Officer and Other Management Succession

One of the most important functions of the board is selecting and assessing the CEO and planning for CEO and other executive officer management succession. Ongoing planning for what happens in the event of a vacancy in leadership is a critical board responsibility. The nominating and governance committee should be prepared and qualified to lead this process.

> *One of the most important functions of the board is selecting and assessing the CEO and planning for CEO and other executive officer management succession. Ongoing planning for what happens in the event of a vacancy in leadership is a critical board responsibility.*

The choice of a new CEO is fundamental to the direction of the company. The CEO is primarily responsible for implementing the corporation's strategic vision with input and guidance from the board. The CEO is also responsible for the short- and long-term performance of the corporation. The CEO will establish in large part the "tone at the top" for legal compliance and ethical standards. Finally, the CEO is generally responsible for the selection and direction of other members of senior management. Consequently, the board must select and continually assess the CEO with care and due consideration for the challenges facing the corporation. The board must monitor the CEO's performance and determine when there is a need for a change in senior management in light of executive performance and the corporation's challenges.

The nominating and governance committee often has the responsibility to recommend to the board a selection process or a successor to the CEO in the event of retirement or termination of service. The committee may also review and approve proposed changes in other senior management positions, with the understanding that the CEO should have considerable discretion in selecting, retaining, and reviewing members of the management team. In order to perform these functions, the committee, or another board committee should, at least annually, review the performance of the CEO and members of senior management.

Succession planning is a continuous board activity that is closely related to management development. The board should be aware of, and regularly reassess, how long the current CEO is likely to continue, what developments may cause a change in that expectation (including a shift in strategy, a change in performance, or an emergency or crisis). The board should also consider what might cause the CEO or other senior executive officers to consider leaving the company. Although all of these factors are relevant, succession planning is in fact a continuous process and one that, by definition, rarely results in a hard and fast plan for a specific outcome. As a result, two key components of succession planning are assessing and developing other management talent and considering what steps the CEO and other senior executive officers can take to further develop their own leadership capabilities and those of their direct reports.

Decisions about succession planning and management development should be closely related to corporate strategy, because the leadership group must have both a clear understanding of the corporate strategy and the ability to implement it. In addition, the committee should ensure the succession plan includes emergency procedures for management succession in the event of the unexpected death, disability, or departure of the CEO. The plan should also incorporate a review, with the CEO, of management's plans for the replacement of members of the senior management team, as well as the CEO's assessment of the ability of team members to lead, whether on an interim or longer basis, should the CEO be incapacitated.

G. Other Committee and Corporate Governance Functions

As mentioned previously, the nominating and governance committee has increasingly assumed responsibility for ensuring that the corporation has adopted, maintained, and regularly updated principles and policies of corporate governance. In addition to addressing director nomination or renomination, committee membership, and management evaluation and succession, the committee typically addresses the following tasks and issues:

- developing, recommending to the board, and monitoring a statement of corporate governance principles or guidelines (required of listed companies by NYSE);
- developing proposals for amendments to bylaws and other governance documents;
- developing policies to respond to shareholder proposals;
- evaluating the effectiveness of individual directors, the board, and board committees (also required by NYSE);
- evaluating director standards of independence and monitoring director compliance with those standards;
- providing for director orientation and education programs;
- reviewing the board's leadership structure;
- reviewing the board committee structure, including each committee's recommendation regarding its charter and size and the possible addition of other committees, such as finance, public policy, or risk management committees;

- reviewing and making recommendations with respect to the corporation's director policies, such as compensation, retirement, indemnification, and insurance;
- examining board meeting policies, such as meeting schedule and location, meeting agenda, presence and participation of non-director senior executives, and materials distributed in advance of meetings; and
- establishing and overseeing procedures for shareholder communications with directors.

H. Board Leadership

As discussed in Section 5 above, many companies that do not have an independent non-executive board chair often designate an independent director as a presiding or lead director or another designation indicating a leadership role among independent directors. This director can be a helpful counterweight to a strong CEO and can ensure that there is an appropriate flow of information to all board members. The nominating and governance committee should consider the appropriateness of such a designation, and if it concludes that it should propose a candidate, it should do so, along with a description of responsibilities. In many cases, the chair of the nominating and governance committee may be the appropriate person for this leadership role. Federal securities laws and regulations require companies to disclose their board leadership structure and the rationale for it.

I. Director Compensation

Either the nominating and governance committee or the compensation committee should periodically evaluate the form and amount of director compensation and make a recommendation to the board about it. The committee can seek the advice of outside compensation consultants to assist it. Directors have an unavoidable conflict of interest in fixing their own compensation, and they cannot eliminate the conflict by having management or a compensation consultant suggest the programs. Directors nevertheless have the responsibility to determine their own compensation, so they must ensure they have considered the information necessary to reach a fair decision, including data on peer companies and an analysis of any factors relating to their particular circumstance, such as the complexity of the company and the expected time commitment.

Director compensation programs should align the directors' interests with the long-term interests of the corporation. Director compensation may take a number of different forms, including annual stock or cash retainers, attendance fees for board and committee meetings, deferred compensation plans, stock options, and restricted stock grants. Additional compensation for additional service, such as for serving as chair of a committee, serving on an *ad hoc* special committee, or serving on a particularly active committee, is also common. There is, however, a trend away from fees for individual meetings. The corporation's executives generally do not receive additional compensation for board service.

SEC proxy disclosure rules require detailed disclosure of all elements of director compensation, including perquisites and charitable donation programs. Any non-monetary items, such as stock options or restricted stock grants, require estimates. Any consulting or other agreements with directors and any payments to directors for consulting or other services beyond the regular directors' fees can impair independence and require disclosure in the annual proxy statement.

The board should be sensitive to and avoid compensation policies or corporate perquisites that might impair the independence of its non-management directors. To maintain directors' focus on proper long-range corporate objectives, most corporations now pay some component of compensation in the form of restricted stock grants and, although there is a shift away from them toward other equity, stock options. The rationale is that these forms of equity compensation strengthen the directors' interest

> *The board should be sensitive to and avoid compensation policies or corporate perquisites that might impair the independence of its non-management directors.*

in the overall success of the corporation and better align their personal interests with those of shareholders. Options alone do not involve acceptance of any economic risk by a director. Therefore, some companies require directors to purchase a minimum amount of stock in the open market or to accept at least a designated portion of their compensation in stock grants rather than cash. In addition, some companies have policies requiring directors to hold, for a minimum period, shares resulting from the exercise of stock options (less sales necessary to fund option exercise and pay commissions and taxes). Although directors' retirement arrangements, insurance policies, and educational or charitable gift programs were once widespread, the increasing perception is that they are not related to corporate performance. As a result, their role in compensation has been reduced or discontinued.

Relationship Between the Board of Directors and Shareholders

A. Nature of the Board/Shareholder Relationship

Shareholders have become more engaged in recent years in the exercise of their rights, particularly their right to elect directors and to participate in annual and special shareholder meetings. Institutions, rather than individuals, are the primary shareholders of large and midsize public corporations, and many of these institutions owe fiduciary duties to their own investors or beneficiaries, which may include exercising their voting rights. Some of these institutions seek to influence the boards of public corporations on key governance decisions, viewing governance advocacy as a tool to improve portfolio performance. Hedge funds have also engaged in shareholder activism to promote a strategy or outcome consistent with their economic interests. The removal of regulatory barriers to communication and coordination among shareholders and the ease of communication in the Internet age have aided shareholders who seek to engage in advocacy, persuasion, and other forms of activism. Moreover, institutions often rely on proxy advisory firms in whole or in part, and this has increased the influence of these firms in voting decisions.

Although the shareholder base of a public corporation is typically a fluid mix of unaffiliated investors with varying interests, the board has the duty to act in the best interests of all shareholders, no matter who nominated the director or the director's affiliation. Shareholders are concerned about a wide variety of corporate governance issues, including the qualifications and composition of the board, executive compensation, financial reporting, the structure of the director election process (*e.g.,* majority voting, proxy access, and the like) and related charter and bylaw provisions (*e.g.,* staggered board and special meeting provisions), other defensive measures (*e.g.,* rights plans), and board leadership (including the question of whether to split the positions of board chair and CEO). Shareholders may submit proposals to the company with regard to one or more of these issues, seeking to change current corporate governance policies. The proposals may be either binding (like bylaw amendments consistent with shareholder rights) or nonbinding. Although shareholders may not have uniform views about any particular governance issue, such proposals, even if advisory, sometimes garner significant shareholder support despite management opposition.

Shareholder advisory firms have policies on a variety of corporate governance issues and publish ratings of a corporation's governance based on the perceived compliance with the advisory firm's policies. These policies often change over time, requiring a continued focus on current governance trends. The advisory firms also recommend votes against directors, or in favor of a "withhold" vote, if the corporation's policies are inconsistent with the advisory group's established positions on a particular matter. Indeed, shareholder advisory firms often support shareholder proposals, and in the event the advisory proposals pass, but are not implemented by the corporation, the firms have recommended a vote against the directors in future elections.

Boards may want to address many of the governance issues of concern to shareholders on their own initiative before being pressured to do so. In assessing governance trends and shareholder proposals, boards must exercise their business judgment, adopt governance changes or improvements appropriate for their company given its circumstances, and resist governance changes that are inappropriate for the company.

Boards may also want to develop communication policies or protocols to promote dialogue with or facilitate receipt of input from shareholders. For example, shareholder groups may request an audience with the lead director, the independent directors, or an independent board committee to discuss various corporate governance issues and concerns. Boards need to consider appropriate policies to respond to such requests. Some boards meet with certain key shareholders from time to time to listen to their views and concerns. These efforts should augment but not replace efforts to ensure that shareholders are informed of the company's efforts toward achieving long-term goals and strategic objectives. The annual meeting also serves as an occasion for information gathering

Some boards meet with certain key shareholders from time to time to listen to their views and concerns. These efforts should augment but not replace efforts to ensure that shareholders are informed of the company's efforts toward achieving long-term goals and strategic objectives.

and outreach to shareholders, and some boards encourage directors to engage shareholders in that environment. In moments of crisis, the board may also need to communicate directly to shareholders.

In any communications or meetings with shareholders, boards must consider confidentiality requirements and Regulation FD compliance, as well as the corporation's disclosure posture on various issues. Moreover, the board must keep in mind that the executive officers of the company carry out the day-to-day management. The CEO or other designated officer should generally be the spokesperson for the corporation on topics relating to the corporation's business, to assure that the corporation conveys a consistent message. Finally, directors must remember that the board acts only as an entity, and any communication policy should consider how to ensure that the board's views are conveyed with one consistent voice.

B. Election Process

As noted above, once elected by the shareholders (or otherwise appointed to the board), directors have a duty to act in the best interests of the corporation to the exclusion of their own interests. Directors are accountable to the corporation's share-holders who, if dissatisfied with the directors' performance, can, depending on state law and the articles or certificate of incorporation and bylaws, vote against reelection (or withhold votes as a protest) or, in cases where the articles and bylaws allow, remove directors from office even before their terms are over.

Directors generally serve for a one-year term or, if a corporation's articles or certificate of incorporation provide for a classified or "staggered" board, for longer. Typically, directors on a classified board serve for staggered three-year terms. The principal benefit of a classified board is to ensure continuity of leadership. In recent years, shareholder activists have criticized classified boards. Classified boards can operate as a takeover defense, because, for example, under some state statutes directors on a classified board can be removed only for "cause" unless otherwise provided in the articles or certificate of incorporation. As a result, it may be difficult for shareholders to unseat directors in the period between elections. As with most aspects of corporate governance, there is no single answer as to the appropriateness of a classified board.

Traditionally, directors have been elected by a plurality vote, which means that the candidates with the highest number of votes in their favor are elected, up to the maximum number of directorships up for election. This standard ensures a successful election. Plurality voting is gradually losing ground as the predominant standard for uncontested director elections as many boards, including a significant percentage of the Fortune 100, have adopted a majority voting standard.

Plurality voting is gradually losing ground as the predominant standard for uncontested director elections as many boards, including a significant percentage of the Fortune 100, have adopted a majority voting standard.

uncontested director elections as many boards, including a significant percentage of the Fortune 100, have adopted a majority voting standard. There are numerous possible formulations of majority voting but, in general, under a majority voting standard a candidate must garner more votes cast in favor than against. Many companies have adopted majority voting, either in their articles or certificate of incorporation or bylaws or as a board policy (which retains plurality voting as the underlying standard for election, but requires candidates who fail to receive a majority of the votes cast to tender their resignation to the board). Plurality voting continues to apply to contested elections.

Boards implementing a form of majority voting need to consider the possible consequences of a majority against/withheld vote, including mechanisms to ensure that the board continues to be able to function effectively in the face of that vote. Most corporations adopting majority voting seek to retain some flexibility for the board through application of holdover rules and policies to allow the independent directors of the board to determine whether to allow the director to continue to serve. Of course, the board must act in the best interests of the corporation and its shareholders in making this decision.

The vast majority of elections for corporate directors are not contested. Incumbent directors (in many cases on recommendation by a nominating committee of the board) choose and nominate a slate and recommend that the shareholders vote for it. Although shareholders have the right to nominate their own candidates, the solicitation of proxies from other shareholders is typically necessary in order for such candidates to have any chance of being elected. This solicitation must comply with the SEC's proxy solicitation rules, including the filing and dissemination of separate proxy materials. The process can be relatively expensive and time-consuming. Further, the outcome of a proxy contest is uncertain, and there are no guarantees that replacement directors will perform any better than the incumbents. Therefore, election contests, even the running of one or two directors (a so-called short slate), are not lightly—or very often—undertaken.

In recent years, shareholders have relied increasingly on "withhold the vote" or "vote against" campaigns to signal disapproval of board candidates or of board policies, instead of seeking to run and elect alternative nominees. These negative campaigns can be powerful catalysts for change. Although the results do not affect the legal outcome of the election in a plurality vote system when there are no competing candidates, there have been some prominent instances in which a large percentage of "withheld" or "against" votes from one or more candidates were followed by a change in the board composition, including the resignation of the affected candidates. Recent changes in law may facilitate contested director elections using only the corporation's proxy materials, in effect making the corporation's proxy a "universal proxy." One purpose of these changes is to address the issues of expense and complexity that make a full proxy contest relatively rare, as noted above. The changes also seek to make it easier for shareholders to promote the election of one or more directors in opposition to the corporation's director nominees. Thus, for example, Delaware law permits a corporation to adopt a bylaw to facilitate a shareholder's access to the proxy statement, and subject to conditions specified in the bylaw, require the corporation to include in its proxy materials one or more nominees submitted by shareholders. The bylaws may limit this right to a minimum level of record or beneficial stock ownership and may also include other conditions such as the number or proportion of directors nominated by a shareholder or whether the shareholder has previously sought to require inclusion of its nominees. Delaware law also permits bylaws to reimburse shareholders' proxy expenses subject to established conditions. The Corporate Laws Committee has adopted similar changes to the Model Business Corporation Act. Finally, pursuant to the Dodd-Frank Act, the SEC has adopted proxy access rules, which, if they become effective, will provide a single federal standard on proxy access to which the state law provisions of Delaware and other states will become complementary.

> *In recent years, shareholders have relied increasingly on "withhold the vote" or "vote against" campaigns to signal disapproval of board candidates or of board policies, instead of seeking to run and elect alternative nominees. These negative campaigns can be powerful catalysts for change.*

Duties Under the Federal Securities Laws

Federal and state laws regulate the disclosure practices and securities transactions of public companies and their directors, officers, and employees. The federal securities laws are administered by the SEC and affect many daily activities of public companies. Violation of these laws may result in significant civil and criminal penalties, imposed not only on the corporation, but also potentially on individual directors and officers. Directors need to be particularly attentive to their own, as well as the corporation's, compliance with these laws. Review of programs and policies designed to maintain compliance with the federal securities laws, absent assignment of responsibilities to a legal compliance committee, is often delegated to the audit committee.

A corporation must maintain effective systems of internal controls and procedures for collecting, reviewing, and disclosing financial and other material information about the corporation. Quarterly review and certification of the effectiveness of systems and procedures that support SEC filings are required of the CEO and the CFO of public companies. Annual evaluation of internal controls over financial reporting by management and attestation of internal controls over financial reporting by the external auditor are also required for many companies. The board, generally through its audit committee, should receive and examine reports concerning each of these reviews.

A. SEC Reporting Requirements

Public companies must file both periodic and current reports with the SEC. Periodic reports include an annual report on Form 10-K and quarterly reports on Form 10-Q. Current reports on Form 8-K are required for disclosure of quarterly earnings releases, material contracts, changes in the board and management, shareholder meeting voting results, and a broad spectrum of other specified events. A Form 8-K may also be used for voluntary disclosure of information. The SEC's proxy rules require that the annual meeting proxy statement be accompanied or preceded by an annual report to shareholders. Many of these reports must include specified financial and other information.

The corporation's annual report on Form 10-K contains the last fiscal year's audited financial statements, as well as risk factors, management's discussion and analysis of the corporation's results of operation and financial condition, and important trends and uncertainties. The Form 10-K is the most detailed of the reports filed with the SEC, and it must be signed by a majority of the corporation's directors. Separate and apart from the audit committee's involvement, all directors should review and be satisfied with the corporate processes used to prepare the Form 10-K and understand the significant disclosures in that report. Therefore, the full board should have an opportunity to read, comment on, and ask questions about the Form 10-K before it is filed.

The audit committee and the board should be satisfied that there are disclosure controls and procedures in place reasonably designed to achieve the timeliness, accuracy, and completeness of annual and quarterly reports, as well as all other reports and public releases.

Directors are not expected to verify independently the accuracy of underlying facts contained in earnings releases or reports filed with the SEC, but they should be satisfied that the disclosures are not contrary to the facts as they know them. In addition, the audit committee and the board should be satisfied that there are disclosure controls and procedures in place reasonably designed to achieve the timeliness, accuracy, and completeness of annual and quarterly reports, as well as all other reports and public releases. In addition, the CEO and CFO of public companies are required to review and, based on their knowledge, certify the material accuracy and completeness of quarterly and annual reports. Quarterly assessments of disclosure controls and procedures and annual assessments of internal control over financial reporting are also required. Audit committee members of public companies should be familiar with these certifications and assessments and the procedures undertaken to support them, and the audit committee should always be attentive to reports of control deficiencies, especially material weaknesses, and be satisfied with management's classification of items as significant deficiencies rather than as material weaknesses.

B. Proxy Statements

Public companies soliciting proxies for shareholder votes on the election of directors or other matters must furnish each shareholder with a proxy statement. In most cases, the company files only the final proxy statement, as distributed. In other cases, if actions other than election of directors or other routine business are to be taken, the company must file a preliminary proxy statement with the SEC, which will often review and clear it. Directors should be attentive to the procedures followed in preparing the corporation's proxy statements. It is good practice for every director to review a reasonably close-to-final draft of the proxy statement before it is distributed or filed with the SEC, particularly sections dealing with matters about which the director has personal knowledge or containing a report of a committee on which the director serves. Similar disclosure requirements can apply when corporate action is being taken without soliciting proxies.

The proxy statement for the annual shareholder meeting must include information about the company's directors, officers, and principal shareholders, as well as about certain of its governance policies. With respect to directors in particular, the proxy statement must include disclosure about each director's and director nominee's experience, qualifications, attributes, or skills that led the board to conclude that the person should serve as a director of the company as of the time the proxy statement is filed with the SEC. It must also include extensive information about the company's compensation of its officers and directors, both in tabular and narrative form, including a detailed discussion of the company's compensation objectives, policies, and practices, as well as information about related person transactions.

C. Fair Disclosure

The SEC's Regulation FD (for "fair disclosure") provides that material information about a public company may not be disclosed on a selective basis by the corporation or its agents to marketplace participants, such as analysts, brokers, investment advisors, and shareholders who may act on the information and have not agreed to keep the information confidential. Rather, the corporation must take steps to disseminate such information in a manner that makes it broadly available to all market participants simultaneously. As a result, directors should be careful not to disclose non-public information about the corporation and its business. Violations of Regulation FD have resulted in SEC enforcement actions and fines against public companies and corporate officers. Regulation FD has caused public companies to adopt more restrictive policies regarding the persons authorized to speak on behalf of the company with securities analysts and others. It has also prompted many companies to make more information public.

D. Registration Statements

Directors should take diligent steps to assure the accuracy of their corporation's registration statements filed with the SEC in connection with any offering (including in a merger or acquisition) of the corporation's securities to the public. Regardless of whether a director actually signs the registration statement, the director is liable for any material inaccuracy or omission in the registration statement, including information incorporated by reference from other filed documents, unless the director establishes that, after due diligence, the director was not aware of the inaccuracy or omission.

The director's primary defense to registration statement liability is due diligence. To establish this defense, the director must show that, after reasonable investigation, the director had reasonable grounds to believe and did believe that the registration statement did not contain any materially false or misleading statements or any material omissions that made the registration statement misleading. Actions required by the director to satisfy the due diligence standard will vary with the circumstances. During the registration process, directors should satisfy themselves that the corporation has developed and used appropriate corporate disclosure controls and procedures reasonably designed to ensure the registration statement's accuracy and completeness. Although all registration statements should be prepared with appropriate care, certain registered offerings may have a higher potential for liability, such as an initial public offering, a follow-on equity offering, a large acquisition using the corporation's equity, or a financing or reorganization of a public company that has experienced problems. Accordingly, a board meeting or meetings with counsel, accountants, and management present at which there is discussion and analysis of the disclosures in the registration statement should precede the filing of registration statements for such offerings.

For many companies, the disclosures in the company's Form 10-K and other reports filed previously with the SEC are incorporated into the registration statement. Therefore, the procedures used to review these reports are important when there is a registered securities offering. Each director also should personally review the registration statement for accuracy, with particular attention to those statements and disclosures in the registration statement that are within the director's knowledge and competence. Directors may also want to consider consulting with the corporation's legal counsel to understand any material changes made to disclosure documents in response to SEC comments and to confirm that the process followed is intended to fulfill the due diligence requirements.

E. Insider Trading

The federal securities laws prohibit corporate insiders, including directors, and the corporation itself from purchasing or selling securities, either in the open market or in private transactions, when they possess non-public, material information about the corporation. The corporation or an insider in possession of such information may not take actions involving the securities until the information is publicly disseminated. Policies should be adopted to address securities transactions, including transactions in 401(k) plans and gifts of securities. The federal securities laws also prohibit insiders from revealing material, non-public information concerning the corporation, or giving a recommendation to buy or sell based upon such information, to others who trade based upon such information. Under the SEC's Rule 10b5-1, directors and other insiders can mitigate the risk of insider trading liability by adopting plans in advance for scheduled sales and purchases of the corporation's securities. As a general rule, the federal securities laws also prohibit the recipient of a tip from acting on material, non-public information obtained from a corporate source.

Information is material if there is a substantial likelihood that a reasonable investor would consider it important in deciding whether to buy, sell, or hold a security. Some believe that information may be considered material if, upon disclosure, it would likely affect the stock price. If there is any doubt whether undisclosed information is material, legal guidance should be sought or, as a practical alternative, the information should be treated as material.

Violation of any of these insider trading laws triggers strict sanctions. The violator is liable for any profit made or loss avoided. In addition, a court can assess a penalty against the trader, the tipper, or the tippee of treble damages—that is, three times the profits made or losses avoided. Criminal sanctions are also possible. The SEC has an aggressive program of discovering and proceeding against insider trading violations. It can award informants who report a violation a percentage of the amount of the penalty recovered. The SEC also can prohibit any individual from serving as an officer or director of any public company if the individual has violated the antifraud or insider trading laws and demonstrates unfitness to serve as an officer or director. In addition to potential violations of federal law, the misuse of confidential corporate information can result in violations of directors' duties under state law, leading to civil lawsuits brought by shareholders.

Many public companies have procedures requiring senior executives and directors to contact corporate counsel, the corporate secretary, or another designated person before trading in the corporation's securities so that any proposed transaction can be reviewed in the light of the current state of public information. Many public companies have policies prohibiting insiders and their affiliates from trading in the corporation's securities during specified "blackout" periods. The board of directors (directly or through its audit or legal compliance committee) should periodically review corporate information disclosure and insider trading policies and procedures in view of Regulation FD (discussed above) and insider trading prohibitions.

F. Reporting Share Ownership and Transactions; Short-Swing Profits

Directors, executive officers, and large shareholders of public companies must report to the SEC all their holdings of and transactions in the corporation's equity securities and must disgorge to the corporation any profits realized from buying and selling (or selling and buying) such securities within any six-month period. Any person who becomes an insider (*e.g.*, a director, executive officer, or more than 10% shareholder) is required to file a report of beneficial ownership and must do so whenever there is a change in beneficial ownership. These reports must be filed on a timely basis. All delinquent filings must be disclosed

Any person who becomes a director, executive officer, or more than a 10% shareholder is required to file a report of beneficial ownership and must do so whenever there is a change in beneficial ownership. These reports must be filed on a timely basis.

in the corporation's annual meeting proxy statement (with the delinquent individuals identified by name), and they can trigger monetary fines. An insider is generally deemed to be the owner of securities that are owned by a spouse or child living with the insider, and may also be deemed to be the owner of securities held in a trust of which the insider is a trustee, settlor, or beneficiary, or of securities owned by a corporation or other entity controlled by the insider.

Profit disgorgement is required if an insider purchases and sells the corporation's securities within a six-month period and vice versa (*i.e.*, sells within six months before buying). Any "profit"—measured as the difference between the prices of any two "matchable" transactions during the six-month period (*i.e.*, the highest priced sale and the lowest priced purchase)—must be paid to the corporation. The requirement is intentionally arbitrary and, subject to tightly defined regulatory exemptions, applies to all transactions within any six-month period regardless of whether the insider had inside information or, in fact, made a profit on an overall basis. This provision is aggressively enforced by a plaintiffs' bar that monitors SEC filings.

Some transactions, such as the grant and exercise of stock options and the acquisition of securities under employee benefit plans, may be exempt from the purchase and sale triggers of the short-swing profit rules if procedural requirements established by SEC rules have been satisfied. Absent an exemption, the receipt of an option, the acquisition of securities through a benefit plan, or the acquisition of a derivative security related to the value of the corporation's common stock normally will be considered to be a purchase of the underlying security and could be matchable against a sale. Unexpected liability may result from the application of the short-swing profit rules. For example, other indirect changes in ownership, such as reclassifications, intra-company transactions, pledges, and mergers, may be considered a purchase or sale transaction for purposes of the short-swing profit rules.

A retiring director may be subject to profit recovery based on transactions occurring during the six months after the director departs. If a director purchases shares of the corporation, resigns, and sells shares within six months after the purchase, liability may be imposed for any short-swing profit even though the individual is no longer a director at the time of the sale.

Directors, officers, and more than 10% shareholders also are prohibited from selling the corporation's shares short; as a means to enforce this restriction, they are required to deliver shares against a sale within 20 days.

This regulatory regime is highly technical. Legal counsel should be consulted before committing to a transaction in the corporation's securities or in options or other derivatives geared to its securities.

G. Sales by Controlling Persons

Unless an exemption is available, the federal securities laws generally require registration with the SEC of the corporation's securities before those securities can be offered or sold to the public by "controlling persons." (Determining who is a controlling person is a complex question of law and fact for which legal guidance is advisable; directors are often considered to be "controlling persons.") The most common exemption is provided by the SEC's Rule 144, which permits the sale of limited amounts of securities without registration if certain conditions are satisfied. Securities acquired by a controlling person in the open market or in a registered offering are subject to the conditions in this rule, which include special filing and disclosure requirements, if they are to be sold to the public.

H. Compliance Programs

Many public companies have established specific policies and procedures dealing with public communications, share ownership reporting, and insider trading. These programs are designed to ensure that the corporation makes complete, accurate, and timely disclosure of material information, complies with the registration requirements, and satisfies other securities law obligations. These programs also help directors and other insiders to comply with insider trading and other applicable laws and the corporation to meet its obligations under Regulation FD to avoid improper selective disclosure of material information. The audit committee (or the legal compliance committee, if there is one) generally should monitor the establishment and operation of such compliance programs.

I.   Directors of Foreign Corporations with Securities Traded in the United States

A large number of non-U.S. corporations file reports with the SEC because their securities are traded on U.S. securities markets or they have a large number of U.S. holders. Traditionally, the federal securities laws have required these "foreign private issuers" to file annual reports and other material information distributed to their shareholders with the SEC but have not otherwise sought to regulate their corporate governance and other internal practices.

The Sarbanes-Oxley Act's reporting and corporate governance requirements generally apply to non-U.S. corporations that have securities registered with the SEC. The SEC, in adopting rules under the Sarbanes-Oxley Act, has considered the concerns of foreign private issuers and made some rules inapplicable to them or included special provisions addressing their concerns. Directors of foreign private issuers should be aware of the general categories of substantive corporate governance requirements that may apply to their corporations.

Liabilities, Indemnification, and Insurance

Directors may incur personal liability for breaches of their duty of care or their duty of loyalty or for failure to satisfy other legal or regulatory requirements, such as the federal securities laws. Corporations may provide for certain limitations on these liabilities, and may also provide directors (and officers) with indemnification rights and insurance. Such provisions allow directors to focus on the creation of value without undue personal risk. Directors should review periodically a corporation's indemnification and insurance as applicable to both directors and officers, in order to ensure that proper consideration has been given to those important issues.

> *Directors may incur personal liability for breaches of their duty of care or their duty of loyalty or for failure to satisfy other legal or regulatory requirements, such as the federal securities laws. Corporations may provide for certain limitations on these liabilities, and may also provide directors (and officers) with indemnification rights and insurance.*

A. Sources of Liability

1. Corporate Law Liability

Corporate law generally provides that directors are fiduciaries and therefore have both a duty of care and a duty of loyalty.

Directors may in theory be liable for violating either of those duties, but nearly every public, and most private, corporations formed in U.S. jurisdictions have, through their charters, precluded monetary liability for directors who breach only the duty of care. Directors should consider whether corporations on whose boards they serve have eliminated such liability.

Directors in most jurisdictions may, however, have monetary liability for breaching the duty of loyalty. Directors can incur liability where they have a conflicting personal interest or are dominated or controlled by a person or entity with such a conflict. Directors should be alert to such conflicts, particularly in corporations with controlling shareholders and in change-in-control transactions where courts are especially sensitive to the duty of loyalty. There are a number of techniques to address these concerns, including disclosure of potential conflicts, recusal of conflicted directors, use of independent committees, and shareholder votes. In addition to liability involving a conflict of interest, directors may also incur liability for breach of the duty of loyalty where their inattention to their duties rises to a level constituting "bad faith" or "conscious disregard for their duties." Good recordkeeping of board procedure and deliberations is important to protecting directors from liability when, in retrospect, business decisions with poor outcomes are alleged to have resulted from conflicts or inattention.

In addition to liability for breach of duties, directors can also be personally liable for authorizing dividends or other distributions, such as stock repurchases, when a corporation is insolvent. This is an area requiring particular caution, because directors may be liable for simple negligence, a lower standard than that typically applicable to liability for breaching fiduciary duties. Accordingly, wherever there is any question as to a corporation's solvency, directors should obtain appropriate advice before making distributions to shareholders.

2. *Federal Securities Law Liability*

As discussed above, directors can be personally liable under the federal securities laws—in some cases even when they act in good faith. In certain circumstances, negligence, by itself, is sufficient to establish liability. In other situations, liability may be imposed, subject only to due diligence or other defenses, without a finding of fault or intent to deceive.

3. Liability Under Other Laws

Directors also can be subject to personal liability under other state and federal statutes, such as environmental laws. Good faith and careful monitoring of management programs directed toward corporate legal compliance (including through periodic briefings on how well the programs are functioning and changes in them) should provide substantial safeguards against any such personal liability.

B. Protections

Several mechanisms help protect directors from personal liability: charter provisions limiting liability, rights to indemnification, advancement of related expenses, and insurance.

1. Limitation of Liability

Most state corporation statutes permit a corporation's charter to include a provision eliminating or limiting the liability of directors to the corporation and its shareholders for monetary damages for breaches of certain duties. The provisions will most frequently eliminate exposure to claims requesting monetary damages for breaches of the duty of care. They do not, however, cover claims for injunctive relief or liabilities to third parties, and they may not be effective to protect a director from liabilities resulting from federal law violations. Generally, these provisions do not protect directors from monetary liability for illegal dividends or stock repurchases, for bad faith actions, for breach of the duty of loyalty, for intentional violations of law or actions where the director received an improper benefit.

2. Indemnification

Most state corporation statutes specify the circumstances in which the corporation is permitted to indemnify directors against liability and to pay related reasonable expenses incurred in defending claims arising in connection with their service as directors.

In general, directors must meet a certain standard of conduct before being indemnified. The standard for permissible indemnification in many state statutes is that the individual director must have acted in good faith and with a reasonable belief that the director's conduct was in (or not opposed to) the best interests of the corporation. In the case of criminal proceedings, the director must also have had no reasonable cause to believe the conduct was unlawful. Such statutes give corporations the power to indemnify directors in actions by third parties, including class actions, for expenses (including attorneys' fees), judgments, fines, and amounts paid in settlement of the actions. In some instances, however, indemnification is not permitted, regardless of the director's standard of conduct. For example, many jurisdictions prohibit indemnification for actual liability in derivative actions.

3. Advancement

In addition to permitting indemnification, state corporation statutes authorize corporations to advance legal fees. For the most part, the limitations on actual indemnification do not apply to advances of legal expenses. Instead, corporate statutes generally permit a corporation to pay a director's legal expenses during the pendency of almost any lawsuit. A director benefiting from such an advance, however, must promise to repay the advance if it is ultimately determined that the director is not entitled to

> *A director benefiting from such an advance, must promise to repay the advance if it is ultimately determined that the director is not entitled to indemnification.*

indemnification. The cost of defending a claim can be substantial, making advancement of expenses important.

4. Mandatory Indemnification and Advancement

State law generally provides corporations with broad discretion to make indemnification and advancement payments, but it provides directors with only limited rights to receive those payments on a mandatory basis. For example, many state statutes provide that indemnification for legal expenses is mandatory when the director has been successful in defending a suit. In order to induce directors to serve, most corporations provide for mandatory indemnification and advancement under certain additional circumstances through provisions in their charters or bylaws or through separate agreements with directors. In many instances, these provisions provide that directors are to be indemnified and advanced expenses to the fullest extent permitted by law. In other cases, the indemnification rights are more limited. Directors should understand the extent of their mandatory rights and any limits on those rights.

5. Insurance

Most corporations purchase directors' and officers' liability insurance covering (i) the corporation for any payment of indemnification and advances for expenses and (ii) directors and officers, if the corporation is unwilling to pay indemnification or advancement obligations (perhaps because of a change in control) or is unable to pay such obligations (perhaps because of insolvency or because the claim is one where indemnification or advancement is not permitted). The relevant statutes of most jurisdictions permit the corporation to pay premiums for this insurance. Because of uncertainty regarding the ability of directors and officers to access policies that also cover the corporation, corporations should consider policies that cover only non-management directors. Such policies often include terms more favorable to the insured than policies that cover both the corporation and its directors.

Certain areas of activity such as environmental, employee benefit, or antitrust matters are often excluded from coverage under a typical directors' and officers' policy. Coverage may also exclude conditions in existence at the time of the application for insurance. Directors' and officers' insurance generally does not cover fraud, criminal penalties, and fines and sometimes excludes punitive damages.

Insurance coverage is not available in every case. Most policies are written on a "claims made" (as compared to an "occurrence") basis, covering only defined claims lodged against directors during a specified period. In addition, the terms of coverage under differing policies are very complex and can vary greatly from insurer to insurer. Moreover, insurance markets change rapidly, and insurers may assert numerous reservations or defenses when claims are made. Therefore, directors are well advised to engage experts, who can also provide knowledgeable insight respecting current market conditions.

Insurance coverage is not available in every case. Most policies are written on a "claims made" (as compared to an "occurrence") basis, covering only defined claims lodged against directors during a specified period.

In short, it is important for directors to understand the types of directors' and officers' insurance a company has, in addition to the amount of coverage. Directors should ascertain the level of expertise of the person within the corporation responsible for negotiating the coverage or, in the alternative, determine whether an outside expert, familiar with current market conditions and policy and claim issues, is assisting in the process. Directors should also take care (as is true in the case of any insurance policy) in completing policy applications and questionnaires and inquire about the insurance provider's reputation for handling insurance claims and its financial strength. This consideration can be more important than premium pricing. Disputes with the insurance carrier as to whether coverage is available when litigation materializes are an unwanted distraction. Directors' and officers' insurance is a complex area, and directors should seek assurance that the corporation's coverage does in fact afford the best protection obtainable in the current marketplace.

Appendix

Online Corporate Governance Resources

Websites and Blogs

Boardroom INSIDER
http://www.boardroominsider.com

Compensation Standards
http://www.compensationstandards.com

The Conference Board Governance Center Blog
http://tcbblogs.org/governance/

Corporate Board Member
http://www.boardmember.com

TheCorporateCounsel.net
(includes Broc & Dave's blog and the Proxy Season blog)
http://www.thecorporatecounsel.net

Corporate Governance
http://www.corpgov.net

The Corporate Library
http://thecorporatelibrary.com

The D & O Diary
http://www.dandodiary.com

DealLawyers.com
http://www.deallawyers.com

Delaware Corporate and Commercial Litigation Blog
http://www.delawarelitigation.com

Deloitte & Touche LLP's Center for Corporate Governance
http://www.corpgov.deloitte.com/site/us/

Directorship
http://www.directorship.com

Financial Accounting Standards Board
http://www.fasb.org

Financial Executives International
http://www.financialexecutives.org

Financial Industry Regulatory Authority
http://www.finra.org

Footnoted
http://www.footnoted.com/

The Harvard Law School Forum on Corporate Governance
and Financial Regulation
http://blogs.law.harvard.edu/corpgov/

NASDAQ Stock Market, Inc.
http://www.nasdaq.com

New York Stock Exchange (including NYSE-Sponsored
Commission on Corporate Governance Report, dated
September 23, 2010)
http://www.nyse.com

Public Company Accounting Oversight Board
http://www.pcaobus.org

Race to the Bottom
http://www.theracetothebottom.org/

RiskMetrics Group/Institutional Shareholder Services
(includes governance exchange available to directors, the Risk
and Governance Blog and Risk and Governance Weekly)
http://www.riskmetrics.com

Romeo & Dye's Section16.net
http://www.section16.net

SEC Actions
http://www.secactions.com

Securities Information
http://www.secinfo.com

Securities Lawyer's Deskbook
http://www.law.uc.edu/CCL/xyz/sldtoc.html

Securities Law Prof Blog
http://lawprofessors.typepad.com/securities/

Securities Mosaic Blogwatch
http://www.knowledgemosaic.com/sm/frames/
FrameOpen.asp?ContentASP=/websitelinks/blogwatch.asp

The 10b-5 Daily
http://www.the10b-5daily.com

U.S. Securities and Exchange Commission
http://www.sec.gov

Academic and Research Centers and Institutes

Arthur and Toni Rembe Rock Center for Corporate Governance, Stanford Law School

The center creates a cross–disciplinary environment where economists, lawyers, financial experts, political scientists, engineers, and practitioners can meet and work together to advance the practice and study of corporate governance. http://www.law.stanford.edu/program/centers/rcfcg/

Carol and Lawrence Zicklin Center for Business Ethics Research, The Wharton School of the University of Pennsylvania

A center for business ethics teaching and research at The Wharton School. The center's website lists its publications, upcoming conferences, and links to online business ethics, corporate governance, and compliance resources. http://www.zicklincenter.net/index.html

Center for Leadership and Change Management, The Wharton School of the University of Pennsylvania

The center conducts research and determines practical application in the area of leadership and change, fosters an understanding of how to develop organizational leadership, and supports global leadership initiatives. Its website has links to corporate governance publications and online resources. http://leadership.wharton.upenn.edu/governance/index.shtml

Corporate Law Center, University of Cincinnati College of Law

The University of Cincinnati College of Law's center focuses on issues of importance to corporate lawyers and administers the Securities Lawyer's Deskbook. The center also conducts an annual corporate law symposium. http://www.law.uc.edu/institutes-centers/corporate-law-center

Corporate Governance Institute, San Diego State University

Hosted at San Diego State University, the institute focuses on identifying "responsible practices" in all aspects of corporate governance.

http://www-rohan.sdsu.edu/dept/corpgov/

Ethics Resource Center

The center is a nonprofit research organization dedicated to advancing high ethical standards and practices in public and private institutions. It provides many services to businesses including assistance in establishing an effective ethics and compliance program.

http://www.ethics.org/

Institute for Business and Professional Ethics, DePaul University

An institute at DePaul University that promotes ethical decision-making in business. The institute's website provides information on upcoming events and links to other resources on the web.

http://commerce.depaul.edu/ethics/

Kennesaw State University Corporate Governance Center

The website of the center contains an extensive list of periodicals and websites related to corporate governance, and the center provides various board advisory services.

http://coles.kennesaw.edu/centers/corporate-governance/

John L. Weinberg Center for Corporate Governance, University of Delaware

The center proposes progressive changes in corporate structure and management through education and interaction. It conducts conferences, workshops, research, publication, and other activities to create a forum for business leaders, members of corporate boards, the legal community, academics, practitioners, and students interested in corporate governance issues.

http://www.lerner.udel.edu/centers/ccg

Lindenauer Center for Corporate Governance, Amos Tuck School of Business Administration at Dartmouth
The center's activities focus on the study of how governance should adapt to increasing global competition.
http://mba.tuck.dartmouth.edu/ccg/

Millstein Center for Corporate Governance and Performance, Yale University
This center at the Yale School of Management provides active support for research in corporate governance and disseminates its work to the world's academic, policy-making, and professional communities.
http://millstein.som.yale.edu/

National Center for Employee Ownership
A nonprofit membership and research organization that provides information on employee stock ownership plans and equity compensation plans.
http://www.nceo.org/

The Pension Research Council of the Wharton School of the University of Pennsylvania
The Pension Research Council is an organization devoted to generating and enhancing the debate on policy issues affecting pensions and other employee benefits.
http://www.pensionresearchcouncil.org/

Associations & Organizations

American Bar Association, Section of Business Law
A membership section of the American Bar Association furthering the development and improvement of business law, educating members in business law and related professional responsibilities, and helping members to serve their clients competently, efficiently, and professionally. The Section of Business Law includes the following:

Committee on Corporate Governance

Committee on Corporate Laws

Committee on Federal Regulation of Securities

Presidential Task Force on Corporate Responsibility

http://www.abanet.org/buslaw/home.shtml

American Management Association
A non-profit, membership organization established to assist individuals and organizations in improving organizational effectiveness.
http://www.amanet.org/

Association of Corporate Counsel
A membership organization of in-house counsel whose members represent attorneys employed by more than 10,000 legal departments of corporations, associations, and other private-sector organizations in 70 countries.
http://www.acc.com/

BoardSource
A nonprofit organization devoted to assisting the board members and executive staff of nonprofit corporations in the performance of their duties.
http://www.boardsource.org/

Business Roundtable
An organization of more than 150 CEOs of America's largest companies that calls for a focus on "substance over form," rejecting a call by some institutional investors for such fixed policies as mandatory retirement ages for directors, outside directors that are completely independent of management, and separation of the roles of CEO and board chair.
http://businessroundtable.org/

CFA Institute
An international association of investment professionals dedicated
to increasing knowledge and professionalism in the field.
https://www.cfainstitute.org

The Conference Board
A business membership and research organization whose
membership includes over 2,900 companies in 65 countries.
The Conference Board conducts a wide range of conferences
and produces a variety of publications. The organization has
a governance center, the website of which includes a blog
providing timely analysis of corporate governance issues and
resources for boards.
http://www.conference-board.org/

Ethics & Compliance Officer Association
An association for individuals responsible for corporate ethics,
compliance and business conduct programs.
http://www.theecoa.org

National Association of Corporate Directors
A membership organization for board members and advisors.
The NACD publishes a variety of reports on corporate
governance, as well as a monthly newsletter.
http://www.nacdonline.org/

National Association of Public Pension Attorneys
A provider of educational opportunities and informational
resources for attorneys representing public pension funds.
http://www.nappa.org/

National Association of Stock Plan Professions
An association with 6,000 members whose purposes is to meet
the needs of stock plan professionals whose responsibilities
relate to stock plan design and administration, including
compensation and human resources professionals, stock plan
administrators, securities and tax attorneys, accountants,
compensation consultants, corporate secretaries, transfer agents,
stock brokers, and software vendors.
http://www.naspp.com

National Investor Relations Institute
An association of over 4,000 corporate officers and investor
relations consultants from 2,000 public companies. The institute
produces a monthly newsletter and quarterly magazine, as well
as conducts a variety of seminars and conferences every year.
http://www.niri.org/

Society of Corporate Secretaries and Governance Professionals
An association of corporate secretaries whose membership
represents over 2,500 private, public, and not-for-profit
corporations in the United States.
http://www.governanceprofessionals.org/

Social Responsibility

Business for Social Responsibility
A membership organization designed "to develop sustainable
business strategies and solutions" in the areas of the
environment, human rights, economic development, and
governance and accountability.
http://www.bsr.org/

Caux Round Table
An international group of business leaders that promotes moral
capitalism using sustainable and socially responsible business
practices. The CRT's *Principles of Business* is available online in
twelve different languages.
http://www.cauxroundtable.org/

Dow Jones Sustainability Indexes
Six indexes that track the financial performance of the leading
sustainability-driven companies, with the global index covering
the top 10% of the biggest 2,500 companies in the world.
http://www.sustainability-index.com/

Interfaith Center for Corporate Responsibility
The center has 275 faith-based institutional investor members,
including national denominations, religious communities,

pension funds, foundations, hospital corporations, asset management companies, colleges, and unions, and seeks to integrate social values into corporate and investor actions. The website lists and has links to shareholder proposals submitted for annual meetings.
http://www.iccr.org/

SocialFunds.com
News, information, research, investment analysis and financial services for socially responsible investors.
http://www.socialfunds.com/

Social Investment Forum
The Social Investment Forum is a membership organization for professionals, firms, institutions and organizations that advances socially responsible and sustainable investing.
http://www.socialinvest.org/

Institutional Investors

AFL-CIO
A voluntary federation of 56 national and international labor unions, with over 11.5 million members.
http://www.aflcio.org

American Federation of State, County and Municipal Employees
Union with 1.6 million members in various public service jobs.
http://www.afscme.org/

Ipreo: Bigdough.com
Bigdough.com contains a searchable database of global institutional money managers and their stock holdings.
http://www.bigdough.com/

California Public Employees' Retirement System (CalPERS)
The California Public Employees' Retirement System is the
nation's largest public pension fund. The website includes
links to the websites of approximately 40 other public pension
systems.
http://www.calpers.ca.gov/

Council of Institutional Investors
This is a nonprofit association organization of over 140 large
public, union, and corporate pension funds. The council
advises its institutional shareholder members about corporate
governance, shareowner rights, and other investment issues
to help them protect pension plan assets and seeks to be a
prominent voice for institutional shareholder interests.
http://www.cii.org/

Investment Company Institute
The Investment Company Institute is a national association
of investment companies, and its membership includes over
7,000 mutual funds. The institute encourages adherence to
high ethical standards; advances the interests of funds, their
shareholders, directors, and investment advisors; and promotes
public understanding of mutual funds and other investment
companies.
http://www.ici.org/

Teachers Insurance and Annuity Association – College
Retirement Equities Fund (TIAA-CREF)
TIAA-CREF is the nation's largest retirement system, with
over 2 million members from academic, medical, cultural, and
research institutions. It provides its members with financial
products and services and monitors corporate governance
policies to protect its members' retirement assets.
https://www.tiaa-cref.org

United Brotherhood of Carpenters and Joiners of America
North America's largest building-trades union, with more than
a half-million members in the construction and wood-products
industries.
http://www.carpenters.org

Retail Investors and Investor Suffrage Movement

Investor Suffrage Movement
http://www.isuffrage.org

Moxy Vote
http://www.moxyvote.com

ProxyDemocracy
http://www.proxydemocracy.org

Shareholder Communications Coalition
http://www.shareholdercoalition.com/

ShareOwners.org
http://www.shareowners.org

Transparent Democracy
http://transparentdemocracy.org

VoterMedia Finance Blog
http://votermedia.wordpress.com/

International Resources

Asian Corporate Governance Association
The association is an independent, non-profit membership
organization dedicated to working with investors, companies
and regulators to implement effective corporate governance
practices throughout Asia.
http://www.acga-asia.org/

Berlin Center of Corporate Governance
The center is an empirical research center that performs
systematic surveys of the corporate governance practices of
German companies.
http://www.bccg.tu-berlin.de/

British Accounting Association: Special Interest Group on
Corporate Governance, Cardiff Business School
The group's purpose is to serve as a forum for research and
dialogue on corporate governance issues and to bring together
academics and professionals to discuss their research and the
latest developments in international corporate governance.
http://www.cardiff.ac.uk/carbs/research/groups/cgsig.html

Canadian Coalition for Good Governance
The Coalition was formed to promote good governance
practices in companies owned by its members. Generally, these
companies are members of the S&P/TSX Composite Index.
The Coalition's members are institutional investors: pension
funds, mutual funds, and third party money managers
(currently 41 members managing over $1.4 trillion in assets).
http://www.ccgg.ca/

Canadian Corporate Governance Institute
The institute researches all aspects of Canadian corporate
governance to help Canadians become informed about
the laws, regulations, economic issues, and policy debates
surrounding corporate governance. It studies governance of
listed corporations, family firms, public sector enterprises, and
not-for-profit organizations.
http://www.business.ualberta.ca/Centres/CCGI.aspx

Centre for Corporate Governance Research, Birmingham
Business School
The centre researches the relationship among directors,
investors, and other stakeholders, voting trends, and other
corporate governance developments in the United Kingdom
and internationally.
http://www.business.bham.ac.uk/research/accounting/ccgr/

Corporate Governance Japan
The site is an on-line forum that promotes broader
understanding and lively debate about the ongoing process of
change within Japanese corporations.
http://www.rieti.go.jp/cgj/en/index.htm

Clarkson Centre for Business Ethics + Board Effectiveness
The CCBE is located at the Rotman School of Management
at the University of Toronto. It monitors Canadian corporate
governance trends and provides guidance to firms looking to
improve their board effectiveness and disclosure.
http://www.rotman.utoronto.ca/ccbe/

European Commission: Modernization of Company Law and
Enhancement of Corporate Governance
The communication explains why the European regulatory
framework for company law and corporate governance needs
to be modernized and proposes several initiatives to achieve
this modernization.
http://ec.europa.eu/internal_market/company/modern/
index_en.htm

European Corporate Governance Institute
The institute is an international scientific non-profit association
that provides a forum for debate and dialogue between
academics, legislators, and practitioners, focusing on major
corporate governance issues and best practices. The institute's
website includes links to corporate governance laws and
regulations for numerous countries.
http://www.ecgi.org/

Global Corporate Governance Forum
The forum is joint project between World Bank and
Organisation for Economic Co-operation and Development and
supports regional and local initiatives to improve corporate
governance in middle- and low-income countries in the context
of broader national or regional economic reform programs.
http://www.gcgf.org/

Hermes Pensions Management Limited
Hermes is a UK-based organization that provides asset and
pension fund management services and advises on responsible
investing. Its website discloses its pension fund voting history.
http://www.hermes.co.uk/

Hong Kong Institute of Chartered Secretaries
An organization to support and educate chartered secretaries in
Hong Kong companies on corporate governance, compliance,
and other legal developments related to chartered secretaries'
responsibilities.
http://www.hkics.org.hk/

Institute for International Corporate Governance and
Accountability
The institute studies corporate governance systems and capital
markets throughout the world and develops methods to devise
and sustain responsible and accountable corporate behavior.
http://128.164.132.19/iicga/who.asp

Institute of Corporate Directors
The mission of this institute is to represent the interests of
directors – to foster excellence in directors to strengthen the
governance and performance of Canadian corporations.
http://www.icd.ca/

Institute of Directors
An organization of about 45,000 directors in the United
Kingdom that provides its members with information on local
and international corporate governance members and best
practices related to their duties and responsibilities as directors.
http://www.iod.com

Institute of Directors Southern Africa
The institute is committed to the development of directors,
continuous board learning and improving board effectiveness
by providing members ongoing educational opportunities,
technical advice, leadership publications and updates featuring
the latest developments in corporate governance, as well as
unique networking opportunities.
http://www.iodsa.co.za/

International Association for Business and Society
An association composed of academics and practitioners that
researches relationships between business, government, and
society. The association's website contains information on
upcoming conferences, links to its *Business and Society* journal
and copies of its newsletter.
http://iabs.net/

International Centre for Corporate Social Responsibility,
Nottingham University Business School
This center conducts interdisciplinary and cross-border
research on corporate social responsibility, governance, and
accountability issues.
http://www.nottingham.ac.uk/business/ICCSR/

International Corporate Governance Network
The network is a global membership organization of around 450
leaders in corporate governance based in 45 countries with a
mission to raise standards of corporate governance worldwide.
http://www.icgn.org/

Organisation for Economic Co-operation and Development
The organization provides a setting where governments
compare policy experiences, seek answers to common
problems, identify good practice, and coordinate domestic
and international policies. Thirty-three countries are
members of the organization.
http://www.oecd.org/home/

Proxinvest
Proxinvest is an independent French proxy voting advisory
company that provides services exclusively to investors, large
and small, using methods that promote shareholder interests.
http://www.proxinvest.com

SHARE
SHARE is a Canadian proxy advisory firm focused on environmental, social and governance issues. It makes research, including with respect to shareholder proposals, available on its website.
http://www.share.ca/

Social Investment Organization: The Canadian Association for Socially Responsible Investment
A nonprofit membership organization composed of financial institutions, investment firms, financial advisors, and other organizations and individuals interested in socially responsible investment in Canada.
http://www.socialinvestment.ca/

United Kingdom Institute of Chartered Secretaries and Administrators
The institute is the international qualifying and membership body for the chartered secretary profession. Its members help shape the governance agenda and promote the best practices essential for organizational performance.
http://www.icsa.org.uk

United Kingdom Institute of Directors
The institute is a non-party political business organization with around 55,000 members, including directors from many sectors of the economy—from media to manufacturing, e-business to public sector—and CEOs of large corporations and entrepreneurial directors of start-up companies.
http://www.iod.com/Home/

VIP – Association of Institutional Shareholders
VIP is an international discussion and information platform regarding corporate governance and provides proxy services to institutional investors.
http://www.vip-cg.com/